THE TOP UK AIR FRYER *Cookbook* 2023

Over 150 Delicious & Healthy Traditional British Recipes Using European Measurements + Tips & Tricks for Using Your Air Fryer

VICTORIA ANDERSON

© **Copyright 2022 Victoria Anderson - All rights reserved.**

The content contained within this book may not be reproduced, duplicated, or transmitted without direct written permission from the author or the publisher.

Under no circumstances will any blame or legal responsibility be held against the publisher, or author, for any damages, reparation, or monetary loss due to the information contained within this book. Either directly or indirectly.

LEGAL NOTICE:

This book is copyright protected. This book is only for personal use. You cannot amend, distribute, sell, use, quote or paraphrase any part, or the content within this book, without the consent of the author or publisher.

DISCLAIMER NOTICE:

Please note the information contained within this document is for educational and entertainment purposes only. All effort has been executed to present accurate, up to date, and reliable, complete information. No warranties of any kind are declared or implied. Readers acknowledge that the author is not engaging in the rendering of legal, financial, medical or professional advice.

The content within this book has been derived from various sources. By reading this document, the reader agrees that under no circumstances is the author responsible for any losses, direct or indirect, which are incurred as a result of the use of the information contained within this document, including, but not limited to: errors, omissions, or inaccuracies.

TABLE OF CONTENTS

▪ INTRODUCTION 8
- What is an Air Fryer? 8
- How do air fryers work? 8
- How to use an air fryer 9
- What kind of foods can be cooked in an air fryer? 9
- Air Fryer Tips & Tricks 10
- Cleaning an Air Fryer 11
- Air Fryer FAQ 11
- Final words 11

▪ BREAKFAST RECIPES 15
- Breakfast Burrito 16
- French Toast 16
- Air Fryer Granola 17
- Breakfast Sausages 17
- Breakfast Potatoes 18
- French Toast Sticks 18
- Egg Muffins 19
- Eggs in a Basket 19
- Pizza Omelet 20
- Scrambled eggs 20
- Hash browns 21
- Pizza Rolls 21
- Tortilla Toast 22
- Cinnamon Rolls 22
- Stuffed Peppers 23
- Hot Dogs 23
- Breakfast Egg Tarts 24
- Crispy Egg Cups 24
- Sweet Croissants 25
- Peanut Butter and Jelly French Roast 25
- Hot Dogs with Puff Pastry 26
- Shakshuka 26
- Egg Cups 27
- Bacon-Wrapped Hard-Boiled Eggs 27
- Hard-Boiled Eggs 28
- Eggs and Sausages 28
- Breakfast Pizza 29
- Breakfast Tortilla 29
- Puff Pastry Mini Pies 30
- Stuffed Avocado 30

▪ SNACK / APPETIZER RECIPES 32
- Tortilla Chips 33
- Stuffed Mushrooms 33

Mozzarella Sticks 34
Cauliflower Steaks 34
Stuffed Jalapenos 35
Courgette Fries 35
Courgette Pancakes 36
Crispy Ravioli 36
Roasted Cauliflower 37
Spicy Tofu 37
Cauliflower Cakes 38
Aubergine Fries 38
Spicy Cauliflower Florets 39
Crispy Cheese 39
Aubergine parmigiana 40
Crispy Chickpeas 40
Aubergine Sticks 41
Sticky and Sweet Air Fryer Aubergine 41
Crispy braided tofu 42
Pasta Chips 42
Air Fryer Mushrooms 43
Fried Pickles 43
Braided Asparagus 44
Pepperoni Toasts 44
Asparagus with Bacon 45
Asparagus with Lemon 45
Crab Cakes 46
Garlic Bread 46
Bacon Chips 47
Taquitos 47

■ POTATO RECIPES 49
Potato Fries 50
Spicy Potatoes 50
Crispy Potatoes 51
Classic Air Fryer Potatoes 51
Juicy Air Fryer Potatoes 52
Potato Chips 52
Best Air Fryer Potatoes 53
Potatoes and Cheese 53
Potato Crunchies 54
BBQ Sauce Potatoes 54
Hot Sauce Potatoes 55
Crispy Sweet Potatoes 55
Mashed Sweet Potatoes 56
Sweet Potato Chips 56
Hasselback Sweet Potatoes 57
Smashed Potatoes 57
Sweet Potato Fries 58
Sweet Potato Cakes 58
Sweet Potato Garlic Crisps 59

Sweet Potato Casserole 59
"Grilled" Sweet Potato Slices 60
Hasselback Potatoes 60
Smashed Garlicky Potatoes 61
Domino Potatoes 61
Sweet Potato Tater Tots 62
Potato Balls 62
Cheesy Ranch Baby Potatoes 63
Potatoes and Sausages 63
Hasselback Potatoes the Other Way 64
Bacon and Potatoes 64

■ LUNCHES AND DINNERS RECIPES 66

Hot Chicken Wings 67
Chicken Wings 67
Chicken Parmigiana 68
Roasted Chicken 68
Chicken with Broccoli 69
Garlic Chicken 69
Crispy Chicken 70
Chicken Thighs 70
Chicken in Orange Sauce 71
Chicken Rissoles 71
Chicken Meatballs 72
Crispy Chicken Tenders 72
Chicken Drumsticks 73
Turkey Meatballs 73
Chicken Schnitzel 74
Chicken Nuggets 74
Chicken and Prosciutto 75
Chicken Tandoori 75
Chicken and Veggies 76
Pork Shoulder 76
Soy Sauce Pork Bites 77
Chicken with Brussels Sprouts 77
Juicy Parmesan Crusted Pork Chops 78
Maple Mustard Pork Tenderloin 78
Air Fryer Pork Chops 79
Pork and Veggies 79
Pork with Mushrooms 80
Honey Glazed Pork Ribs 80
Air Fryer Pulled Pork 81
Crispy Air Fryer Pork Belly 81
Steak Bites 82
Air Fryer Steak 82
Air Fryer Flank Steak 83
Juicy Air Fryer Steak 83
Beef and Veggies Skewers 84

◼ VEGAN AND VEGGIES RECIPES 86

Vegan Spaghetti Pie 87
Air Fryer Crispy Tofu Burgers 87
Cherry Tomatoes with Basil Dressing 88
Toasted Veggies 88
Roasted Broccoli with Garlic Vinaigrette 89
Peanut Butter Cauliflower Bites 89
Kale and Potato Nuggets 90
Buffalo Cauliflower 90
Grean Beans with Garlic Mustard Dressing 91
Crispy Tofu 91

◼ DESSERTS RECIPES 93

Mini Apple Pies 94
Easy Brownies 94
Baked Apples 95
Apple Fritters 95
Chocolate Muffins 96
Best Peanut Butter Explosion Cakes 96
Cookies 97
Air Fryer Churros 97
Pancakes 98
Air-Fried Bananas 98
Air-Fried Oreos 99
Caramelized Pineapple 99
Hand Jam Pies 100
Air Fryer Cronuts 100
Air Fryer Apple Fries 101

INTRODUCTION

WHAT IS AN AIR FRYER?

The air fryer is a countertop cooking appliance that circulates hot air thanks to a powerful fan that's built inside the machine. This machine claims to mimic the results of deep-fried food using little-to-no oil – just hot air. Air fryers promote healthy cooking with less fat that are still tasty and crispy. Most recipes turn out crispy on the outside and moist and tender on the inside.

Some people confuse baking with air frying, but these are two different ways of cooking food. This kitchen appliance has become very popular in the last few years, and by now, many UK families have one in their kitchens. It's a tool that makes your cooking more accessible, healthier, and quicker.

There are two main types of Air Fryers: oven air fryers and basket air fryers.

An air fryer oven is similar to a toaster oven and needs more space in your kitchen. It does have more room for food inside and more cooking functions.

Air fryer baskets are more practical and economical. They can fit food for one, two, or even four people. All recipes from this book can be easily made in both types of air fryers, but I will put more accent on the air fryer baskets.

There are several popular brands of air fryers. My top favourites are Phillips, Cosori, Ninja, Vortex, and Gorenje. They range in price depending on their performance, size, and features.

An air fryer is not a deep fryer, even though you get similar results, but in a much healthier way. You can cook your favourite meals without mess or odor.

You can also bake foods – even cookies – in your air fryer. One thing I love about air fryer is that it won't heat your house like an oven will. (This is extremely important to me during the summertime.) The food also come out much quicker than cooked in the oven.

HOW DO AIR FRYERS WORK?

The top of the machine holds a heating machine and a fan. When you turn the air fryer on, hot air rushes down and circulates around the food. The food is placed in an air fryer basket, a container where you put the food you want to cook. The more rapidly the air circulates around the food, the crispier the food will be, creating a fried and crispy exterior without oil (or with just a little oil).

Using an air fryer is easy:

1. Place your food in the air fryer basket. You can put any food you like, and in most cases, you need to add 1 or 2 tablespoons of oil to help the food get nice and crispy on the outside but also tender and juicy on the inside.

2. Set the temperature and time for cooking the food. These usually range from 150°C to 200°C and 5 to 25 minutes, depending on what you are cooking.

3. Let your food cook. Sometimes you need to flip the food to the other side to even up the crispness (e.g., chicken recipes) or shake the basket (potato fries).

Finally, remember to clean your Air Fryer once your food is finished. I will show my foolproof way of cleaning your air fryer like a pro whenever it's messed with greasy foods.

HOW TO USE AN AIR FRYER

You need to know some crucial things before using your Air Fryer. Here's what to have in mind when using this kitchen appliance:

Never, NEVER overcrowd the Air Fryer basket. This is very important if you want crispy fried-like food every time. The food must be in a single layer in the basket. It's better to cook the food in two or more batches than to overcrowd the basket. This will result in much tastier food, and your tastebuds will be thankful. :)

An air fryer is made to air fry the food, not deep fry food. Never fill the air fryer basket with oil. You can drizzle a tablespoon or two on top of your food for much crispier results. This will be more than enough oil if you want to add flavour to the food you are cooking.

Choose the right temperature for the food you are cooking. This is an essential part of using an air fryer. Most air fryers come with instructions on recommended temperatures for different foods. It's okay to follow these. You will only speed up the process if you add some degrees when cooking food. (For example, the maximum recommended temperature for air-frying bacon is 177°C.) You should be aware of the smoking point when air frying bacon. Anything above that will result in smoke, which you don't want when air frying. Be careful of using oils that have low smoking temperatures as well.

Pulling out the air fryer basket, shaking, and flipping the food is okay. This can be done to check the doneness of the food, flipping the food, or shaking food for better cooking. The cooking time will continue when you bring the basket back in the air fryer.

The secret for always crispy and golden-brown food is to always dry your food well before placing it in an air fryer, whether it's chicken, pork, another type of meat, or potato fries. Pat dry the food with kitchen paper or a towel, and then you can add some oil and other seasonings. This will result in a crispy exterior and a tender and juicy interior.

Food can be reheated in an air fryer just like in a microwave. You need to use a temperature about 20 degrees lower than the temperature you will use to cook the food. The time will range from 2-6 minutes, depending on what you reheat; For example, to reheat pizza in your air fryer, heat at 160°C for about 3-4 minutes; to reheat your fries, place them at 177°C for about 3-4 minutes. They will come out perfect and fresh every single time.

WHAT KIND OF FOODS CAN BE COOKED IN AN AIR FRYER?

Cooking in an air fryer doesn't mean you need to make replicas of the best deep-fried recipes. You can cook various recipes in this appliance, from roasting vegetables, making crispy fries, and cooking fish or meat, to making muffins and baking cookies. You can also use frozen foods such as potato fries, mozzarella sticks, chicken nuggets, and fish fingers. The food can be fresh or frozen. You can make finger foods from scratch and cook them in an air fryer just before your guests arrive. Swap regular old-fashioned potato fries with crispy sweet potato fries or even courgette fries.

Did you know that you can even hard boil eggs in an air fryer? It was mind blowing when I discovered that you could easily make a hard-boiled egg in an air fryer.

You must place the raw egg in the basket and turn your air fryer at 200°C for 5 minutes. You can even make a dozen eggs at once!

You can make perfectly cooked chicken that's tender and juicy and always foolproof. Any chicken will work, from wings to drumsticks, from thighs to breasts. I bet you didn't you this, but you can make a whole chicken in an air fryer! Massage it with butter or oil, season it with some of your favourite chicken spices, and turn your air fryer to 180°C for about 40 minutes, flipping the chicken halfway through. You can also air fry pork shoulder, pork chops, fish (braided or plain seasoned with just the simplest of seasonings), and any meatballs you like.

Make your favourite veggies crispy and healthy with some herbs or a sprinkle of parmesan cheese. Or, air fryers are perfect for single-serving desserts like Creme Brulé, muffins, cookies, or even donut holes. Once you try this kitchen appliance, I am sure you will fall in love with it and transform your cooking into something that will become a massive part of your life. If you don't have one, treat yourself this year and cook healthier food for you and the whole family.

AIR FRYER TIPS & TRICKS

Air fryers are great if you live in a small apartment or have limited kitchen space. An air fryer can cook for the whole family. (You may have to cook in batches.)

Air fryers work miracles with many recipes, from breakfasts to yummy lunches or dinners. Here are some tips and tricks you should be aware of:

1. Never air fry battered foods. This might be great for deep frying, but it will cause a mess in your air fryer. Skip doing this because the liquid will spill in the bottom of your air fryer and your food will stick to the basket. In this book, you will find many crispy recipes that are the same as deep fried but without using that liquid batter.

2. Always preheat your air fryer. Preheating your air fryer will ensure and even and crispier cooking than you would experience with your oven. This won't take as much time either because the space is smaller than your oven.

3. Always get that nice golden-brown color for your food. Whether you are cooking frozen food or recipes you make from scratch, ensure you get a lovely and golden finish. The secret to this is oil, but not too much. The trick is to use just a quick mist of a cooking spray to get satisfying results every time.

4. Never overcrowd the basket. Any food will turn into a crispy and golden-brown color if it has enough space inside the basket for the air to circulate. This is one of the crucial keys to always making perfect hamburgers, chicken wings, or even fries.

5. Get even cooking by shaking and flipping the food. This is quite important in some recipes. Shaking will prevent the food from sticking, even up the doneness, and help them get the desired crispness.

6. You don't need to grease and brush the air fryer basket. Even if you cook frozen food, they always tend to have some oil in them, so never touch or grease your air fryer basket. In the same cases, you can spray a little cooking spray on the food to get the perfect crispiness.

7. Use a piece of parchment paper to prevent some foods from sticking. This is only sometimes necessary because the air fryer basket is nonstick. Still, sometimes, when cooking incredibly sticky or delicate food, a piece of parchment paper will help a lot. This will ensure the secure cooking of your food and help you clean up your air fryer much quicker. Nowadays, you can find specialized parchment papers for air fryer baskets in baking stores or easily find them online. Using tin foil will also work with some kinds of foods.

8. In quick and easy steps, you can reheat your leftovers from yesterday's lunch or dinner. Forget about microwaves; use an air fryer to preheat your food leftovers. Warm any food for about 2-6 minutes and serve to enjoy.

9. Give your Air Fryer some space while in use. This means you need to put your air fryer where there are no other kitchen gadgets or appliances next to it. The air needs to circulate, which is essential for this kitchen appliance's healthy use. Place it on the countertop – never on the stovetop – because it will heat a little while it's on, and you don't want to put it anywhere near gas.

10. Use other pans in an air fryer basket. Any baking dish that is good for baking in the oven will also work in an air fryer. These baking dishes can be ramekins, stainless steel pans, silicon pans, and even oven-safe glass pans that are good for microwaves.

11. Hold your food together. This is especially crucial when cooking something wrapped, such as bacon wrapped around something, or a veggie or puff pastry. To hold the food together, use toothpicks. It's always a great way to seal the edges so unfolding doesn't occur.

12. It's okay to open the air fryer basket. This is extremely important in recipes that need to be flipped halfway through cooking. Also, shake the air fryer basket when you want to prevent the food from sticking.

13. Don't discard the juices and sauces from the basket. After cooking chicken or pork tenderloin, the air fryer container will catch all the juices, which are the perfect base for making marinades or gravy. You don't want to throw that away.

There are some mistakes that I see people often make when cooking in an air fryer, such as adding wet food to the air fryer, overcrowding the basket with food, not preheating the air fryer, adding more oil than needed, and repeatedly cooking in a dirty air fryer. It's crucial to wash and clean your air fryer after every cooking.

CLEANING AN AIR FRYER

You've cooked your favourite meal Now it's time to clean your air fryer for future use. Don't be afraid of all the sticky and greasy parts around the air fryer basket. I have a foolproof trick that will help you clean up your appliance much quicker and easier than you think.

One of my favourite ways to clean an air fryer is to fill the basket with water, covering the second basket. I drizzle a little dish soap, turn the basket back in the air fryer and turn the machine to 200ºC for 7 minutes. The hot soapy water will remove all the sticky bits in the basket. Then you need to brush it one last time with a sponge to clean it up thoroughly.

Another way to clean your air fryer is to quickly remove the food bits from the basket and place them in the washing machine.

The most complex way to clean up your air fryer is to let it soak in hot water in your sink for 20 minutes and then wash it thoroughly with a sponge. Let it dry completely before using it again. You don't want any humidity in your food because it will result in your food's crispiness and doneness. You can cook different recipes at a time that are not messy to make, clean, and wipe with a paper towel between each section. This will prevent smoky flavour and give a much better taste to your recipes.

AIR FRYER FAQ

Is air-fried food healthy?

Air-fried is a healthy cooking method because it uses less oil than deep-fried food, but both cooking tastes are the same. For example, French fries prepared in the air fryer have 4 to 6 grams of fat per serving, compared to deep-fried ones, which have up to 17g per serving.

Is an air fryer worth the investment?

Numerous brands sell air fryers nowadays. Investing in a good air fryer that will last much longer is worth it if you enjoy fried food as much as I do. If you don't have a microwave, this will be a 2-in-1 kitchen appliance for you because you can reheat your food too.

Do I need to purchase an extra attachment for my Air Fryer?

Some air fryers have racks, pans, or parchment paper attachments. You don't have to buy all these because you can put the food straight in the basket and cook it until it's done without any fancy or extra equipment. Follow the book's recipes and enjoy them with your loved ones.

How can I prevent a smoky smell when air frying fatty foods?

Dirty air fryers tend to develop a smoky aroma. Foods such as bacon, chicken wings, or pork shoulder can cause a smoky smell. To prevent this, add water to the bottom basket of your air fryer, avoiding smoke.

FINAL WORDS

With this introduction, I have helped you to understand air fryer cooking much more quickly. The recipe selection was difficult because I wanted to cover many creative ways of using this kitchen appliance. This book will offer various recipe ideas for the whole family, from fantastic breakfast ideas to delicious snacks and appetizers for the holidays, from delightful lunch ideas to family full dinner recipes. Finally, remember all the amazing desserts you can prepare with this small but excellent kitchen appliance.

These recipes are foolproof and will never fail you, even if you are a beginner in the kitchen. Let's cook up a storm together.

A group of Chefs trying to make cooking fun and healthy again!

We know how busy you are, that is why we aim to make our recipes as easy, budget friendly and delicious as possible, so you can cook up meals you look forward to that nourish you simultaneously.

With every book we create we also include a Bonus PDF so you get access to coloured images with every single recipe! We couldn't include them in the book due to printing costs and we wanted to keep the books as affordable as possible. We hope you enjoy!

Please email us & our customer support team will help as soon as we possibly can! We want to make sure you are 100% satisfied and if you have any issues at all please email us and we will do our best to help.

Also, if you have any feedback on how we can improve this book & further books please email us that and we will make all the changes we can. As mentioned we can't add colour photos inside the book due to printing costs, but any other improvements we would love to make!

Our customer support email is **vicandersonpublishing@gmail.com** *– as mentioned email us anything you wish here* :)

Happy Cooking!

:)

We hope you enjoy and do let us know your feedback!

Please scan the QR code below to access your bonus PDF with all 150 recipes with full coloured photos & beautiful designs alongside!

This is the only way we can get the recipes with coloured photos to you & keep the book as reasonably priced as possible.

Also, once downloaded you can take the PDF with you digitally wherever you go- meaning you can cook these recipes wherever you may be! (As long as you have an air fryer!)

STEP BY STEP GUIDE TO ACCESS

1. Open Your Phones (Or Any Device You Want The Book On) Back Camera. The Back Camera Is The One You use as if you are taking a picture of someone.
2. Simply point your Camera at the QR code and 'tap' the QR code with your finger to focus the camera.
3. A link / pop up will appear. Simply tap that (and make sure you have internet connection) and the FREE PDF containing all of the coloured images should appear.
4. Now you have access to these FOREVER. Simply 'Bookmark' The tab it opened on, or download the document and take wherever you want.
5. Repeat this on any device you want it on! (If you want it on a laptop, simply email the document to yourself!)

BREAKFAST
Recipes

— 30 RECIPES —

BREAKFAST BURRITO

This breakfast burrito is absolutely amazing. I love to make it for my family whenever I want to fix something quick, easy, and delicious at the same time.

PREPARATION TIME: **10 MINUTES** | COOKING TIME: **10 MINUTES**

SERVING SIZE: **4 PEOPLE** | PER SERVING: **KCAL: 276; FAT: 18.5G; CARBS: 13.4G; PROTEIN: 14.5G; SUGARS: 1.9G; FIBRE: 1.9G**

Ingredients:

- 4 flour tortillas
- 2 breakfast sausages
- 1 tablespoon olive oil
- 2 large eggs, room temperature
- Salt and pepper to taste
- 1 bell pepper, sliced into stripes
- 4 stripes of bacon, diced

Instructions:

Step 1: Warm the olive oil over medium heat in a nonstick frying pan and place the sausages.
Step 2: Season with salt and pepper to taste. With the help of a wooden spoon, crumble the sausages and brown them for 2-3 minutes.
Step 3: Stir in the diced bacon and bell pepper. Gook for 1-2 more minutes. Set aside.
Step 4: Whisk the eggs with the help of a fork and cook them in the same pan until scrambled.
Step 5: Take each tortilla and place some of the sausage mixture and some of the scrambled eggs. Wrap them into a burrito and put these in an air fryer basket.
Step 6: Cook for about 10 minutes at 160°C.
Step 7: Serve and enjoy.

FRENCH TOAST

This French toast recipe will become your go-to and your breakfast staple. Quick, prepared in minutes, and delicious.

PREPARATION TIME: **5 MINUTES** | COOKING TIME: **10 MINUTES**

SERVING SIZE: **4 PEOPLE** | PER SERVING: **KCAL: 311; FAT: 9G; CARBS: 47.5G; PROTEIN: 9G; SUGARS: 6.7G; FIBRE: 0.2G**

Ingredients:

- 2 large eggs, room temperature
- 2 tablespoons whole milk
- 1 teaspoon vanilla extract
- 2 tablespoons granulated sugar
- ½ teaspoon ground cinnamon
- 8 thick slices of challah bread or brioche bread

Instructions:

Step 1: In a large mixing bowl, whisk the eggs, whole milk, vanilla extract, granulated sugar, and ground cinnamon.
Step 2: Take each piece of challah bread and dip it in the egg mixture.
Step 3: Ensure you drip well before adding it to the air fryer basket.
Step 4: Spray the air fryer basket with cooking spray just a little bit to prevent it from sticking.
Step 5: Cook the French toast at 200°C for about 8-10 minutes.
Step 6: Make sure to flip the bread slices after 5 minutes of cooking and continue until crispy and golden brown for about 3-5 more minutes.
Step 7: Serve on a plate with a drizzle of maple syrup and a dusting of icing sugar if desired.

AIR FRYER GRANOLA

Granola is always best made from scratch. This recipe is quick, mixing everything and toasting it in an air fryer for a couple of minutes. For weeks, you can store this in jars and enjoy it with Greek yoghurt or almond milk.

PREPARATION TIME: 5 MINUTES | **COOKING TIME: 10 MINUTES**

SERVING SIZE: 2 PEOPLE | **PER SERVING: KCAL: 705; FAT: 45.7G; CARBS: 61.5G; PROTEIN: 17.9G; SUGARS: 12.4G; FIBRE: 14.6G**

Ingredients:

- 100g rolled oats
- 40g chopped almonds
- 40g chopped pecans
- 40g chopped hazelnuts
- 30g dried cranberries
- 30g dried cherries
- 2 tablespoons sunflower seeds
- 2 tablespoons flaxseeds
- 1 tablespoon chia seeds
- Pinch of salt
- 1 tablespoon honey
- ½ teaspoon vanilla extract
- 1 teaspoon olive oil
- ¼ teaspoon ground cinnamon

Instructions:

Step 1: In a large mixing bowl, place in the rolled oats, chopped almonds, chopped pecans, chopped hazelnuts, dried cranberries, dried cherries, sunflower seeds, flaxseeds, chia seeds, and a pinch of salt.

Step 2: In another bowl, mix the honey, vanilla extract, olive oil, and ground cinnamon.

Step 3: Drizzle the wet ingredients over the seeds and nuts and toss everything with the help of a spoon.

Step 4: Place the whole mixture in an oven-proof baking dish that will fit in your air fryer basket.

Step 5: Cook at 160°C for about 10 minutes, opening the basket halfway through and tossing everything together, making sure the granola is evenly baked.

BREAKFAST SAUSAGES

These breakfast sausages are healthy alternatives to regular ones. You won't add any extra fat to make them perfectly air fried, and they will become one of your favourite breakfasts.

PREPARATION TIME: 5 MINUTES | **COOKING TIME: 15 MINUTES**

SERVING SIZE: 2 PEOPLE | **PER SERVING: KCAL: 259; FAT: 15.8G; CARBS: 13.1G; PROTEIN: 15.8G; SUGARS: 2G; FIBRE: 2.8G**

Ingredients:

- 4 breakfast sausages
- 2 teaspoons ketchup
- Mayo, sour cream, mustard, or Greek yoghurt for serving
- Black beans, for serving

Instructions:

Step 1: Arrange the breakfast sausages in your air fryer basket, ensuring they don't stick together.

Step 2: Brush them with ketchup with the help of a pastry brush.

Step 3: Turn on the air fryer at 160°C and cook for about 15 minutes.

Step 4: Serve them with mustard, sour cream, mayo, or Greek yoghurt, and enjoy.

BREAKFAST POTATOES

Who said that you couldn't have potatoes for breakfast? This recipe is easy and delicious and will take only 20 minutes to make.

PREPARATION TIME: 5 MINUTES | **COOKING TIME: 15 MINUTES**

SERVING SIZE: 2 PEOPLE | **PER SERVING: KCAL: 344; FAT: 5.2G; CARBS: 69.2G; PROTEIN: 7.6G; SUGARS: 5.5G; FIBRE: 10.8G**

Ingredients:

- 4 potatoes, peeled and sliced into 1 cm pieces
- Salt and pepper to taste
- 1 teaspoon paprika powder
- 1 teaspoon dried oregano
- 1 teaspoon dried dill
- 1 teaspoon onion powder
- ½ teaspoon garlic powder
- 2 teaspoons olive oil

Instructions:

Step 1: In a large mixing bowl, place in the diced potatoes and stir in the seasonings: salt and pepper to taste, paprika powder, dried oregano, dried dill, onion powder, and garlic powder.

Step 2: Drizzle in the olive oil and toss everything until combined.

Step 3: Preheat your Air Fryer for about 2 minutes at 200°C and place the potatoes in the air fryer basket.

Step 4: Reduce the heat to 180°C and cook for about 15 minutes.

Step 5: Shake the air fryer basket halfway through for even cooking. Serve and enjoy.

FRENCH TOAST STICKS

These air fryer French toast sticks are perfect when you want your breakfast to be finger food style. It's delicious and quick to fix, making it an ideal snack for the whole family.

PREPARATION TIME: 5 MINUTES | **COOKING TIME: 10 MINUTES**

SERVING SIZE: 3-4 PEOPLE | **PER SERVING: KCAL: 326; FAT: 6.5G; CARBS: 51.5G; PROTEIN: 15.5G; SUGARS: 21.1G; FIBRE: 6.3G**

Ingredients:

- 2 large eggs, room temperature
- 3 tablespoons whole milk
- 1 teaspoon vanilla extract
- 4 tablespoons granulated sugar
- ½ teaspoon ground cinnamon
- 8 slices of toast bread, sliced in thirds lengthwise

Instructions:

Step 1: In a large mixing bowl, whisk the eggs, whole milk, and vanilla extract.

Step 2: Take each piece of sliced toast bread and dip it in the egg mixture.

Step 3: Ensure you drip well before adding it to the air fryer basket.

Step 4: Spray the air fryer basket with cooking spray just a little bit to prevent it from sticking.

Step 5: Cook the French toast sticks at 200°C for about 5 minutes.

Step 6: Mix the granulated sugar and ground cinnamon in a bowl.

Step 7: Dip the French toast sticks into the sugar-cinnamon mixture and coat them well.

Step 8: Serve on a plate with a drizzle of maple syrup or just as they are.

EGG MUFFINS

If you want gluten-free, delicious, and elegant egg muffins made in an air fryer, you will adore this following foolproof recipe. You can add whatever you desire from your favourite ingredients, but I like to make them with diced ham, cheese, and some jalapeno peppers.

PREPARATION TIME: 10 MINUTES | **COOKING TIME: 15 MINUTES**

SERVING SIZE: 6 MUFFINS | **PER SERVING: KCAL: 194; FAT: 14.8G; CARBS: 1.9G; PROTEIN: 13.5G; SUGARS: 0.7G; FIBRE: 0.5G**

Ingredients:

- 6 large eggs, room temperature
- 3 tablespoons double cream
- Salt and pepper to taste
- 100g cooked ham, diced
- 100g shredded cheese
- 2 jalapeno peppers, diced into smaller pieces
- 2 tablespoons parsley, chopped finely

Instructions:

Step 1: In a large mixing bowl, place the eggs and whisk them together with the double cream.

Step 2: Season with salt and pepper to taste and stir in the diced ham, shredded cheese, and peppers.

Step 3: Finally, stir in the parsley and mix until combined.

Step 4: Spray 6 silicone muffin moulds with cooking spray (not too much) and add some of the egg mixtures.

Step 5: Place the egg muffins in an air fryer basket and cook for about 10-12 minutes at 180ºC.

EGGS IN A BASKET

Cooking eggs in an air fryer is easy and quick, but also perfect for breakfast. These eggs in a basket are fancy and kid-friendly recipes that will make your kids eat healthily and not be picky.

PREPARATION TIME: 5 MINUTES | **COOKING TIME: 10-12 MINUTES**

SERVING SIZE: 1 PERSON | **PER SERVING: KCAL: 329; FAT: 23.1G; CARBS: 10.3G; PROTEIN: 20.1G; SUGARS: 1.7G; FIBRE: 0.5G**

Ingredients:

- 2 medium eggs, room temperature
- Salt to taste
- 1 teaspoon butter
- 2 slices toast bread
- 30g grated cheese
- 1 tablespoon chopped chives, for serving

Instructions:

Step 1: With the help of a round cookie cutter, cut out the middle part of the bread slices.

Step 2: Place a small piece of parchment paper in the bottom of your air fryer basket and brush it with butter.

Step 3: Place the bread slices and crack the eggs in the centre of the bread.

Step 4: Season with salt to taste and sprinkle some grated cheese.

Step 5: Air fry for about 10-12 minutes at 160ºC.

Step 6: Serve with a sprinkle of chopped chives on top and enjoy.

PIZZA OMELET

You will love this omelet recipe because it has the best ingredients for breakfast – pepperoni, cheese, and dried oregano. This makes a huge one-serving portion that will keep you full until lunch.

PREPARATION TIME: 5 MINUTES | **COOKING TIME: 12-15 MINUTES**

SERVING SIZE: 1 PERSON | **PER SERVING: KCAL: 678; FAT: 53.8G; CARBS: 3.8G; PROTEIN: 43.8G; SUGARS: 2.9G; FIBRE: 0.4G**

Ingredients:
- 3 large eggs, room temperature
- 50g pepperoni, diced into smaller pieces
- 50g grated cheese
- ½ teaspoon dried oregano
- Salt and pepper to taste
- 2 tablespoons buttermilk

Instructions:
Step 1: Stir the eggs with the buttermilk in a large mixing bowl.
Step 2: Stir in the diced pepperoni slices, grated cheese, and dried oregano, and season with salt and pepper to taste.
Step 3: Brush a silicon round mold with cooking spray and place it in the air fryer basket.
Step 4: Pour the egg mixture and cook at 160°C for about 12-15 minutes.
Step 5: Serve and enjoy while still warm.

SCRAMBLED EGGS

Did you know that you make perfect scrambled eggs in an air fryer? They are much healthier, and they are ready in around 7 minutes. You can serve them with your favourite spread and a slice of bread.

PREPARATION TIME: 5 MINUTES | **COOKING TIME: 7 MINUTES**

SERVING SIZE: 1 PERSON | **PER SERVING: KCAL: 397; FAT: 31.3G; CARBS: 2.9G; PROTEIN: 26.1G; SUGARS: 2.7G; FIBRE: 0.1G**

Ingredients:
- 2 large eggs, room temperature
- Salt to taste
- 1 teaspoon butter
- 2 tablespoons whole milk
- 50g grated cheese
- 1 tablespoon chives, chopped

Instructions:
Step 1: In a large mixing bowl, whisk the eggs with the salt, whole milk, and grated cheese together.
Step 2: Place a heatproof dish in the air fryer and melt the butter for 1 minute at 180°C.
Step 3: Pour in the scrambled egg mixture and cook for about 3 minutes at 160°C.
Step 4: Open the air fryer basket, stir the eggs, and continue cooking for about 3 more minutes.
Step 5: Serve your scrambled eggs with a sprinkle of chives and enjoy.

HASH BROWNS

Hash browns are perfect for breakfast; with this easy recipe, you will forget about the storebought. With 4 simple ingredients, you can make hash browns from scratch in minutes, and the whole family will love them.

PREPARATION TIME: 10 MINUTES | **COOKING TIME: 20 MINUTES**

SERVING SIZE: 2 PEOPLE | **PER SERVING: KCAL: 314; FAT: 2.8G; CARBS: 67G; PROTEIN: 7.2G; SUGARS: 4.9G; FIBRE: 10.2G**

Ingredients:

- 4 potatoes, scrubbed and shredded
- Salt and pepper to taste
- 1 teaspoon olive oil

Instructions:

Step 1: In a bowl, place the shredded potatoes and season them with salt and pepper to taste.
Step 2: Drizzle some olive oil and mix until combined.
Step 3: Spray your air fryer with a little cooking spray and dump half of the mixture, spreading it all over the basket.
Step 4: Cook for about 15 minutes at 160°C and flip them on the other side to cook for another 5-10 minutes if necessary.
Step 5: Repeat the same process until you use all the hash brown batter.

PIZZA ROLLS

With fresh puff pastry and some other simple ingredients, you can create the best pizza rolls in an air fryer without making a mess in the kitchen. These make the perfect back-to-school ideas that your kids will love. They will take around 20 minutes to cook and about 10 to prepare them.

PREPARATION TIME: 10 MINUTES | **COOKING TIME: 20 MINUTES**

SERVING SIZE: 2 PEOPLE | **PER SERVING: KCAL: 838; FAT: 58.2G; CARBS: 59.4G; PROTEIN: 19.9G; SUGARS: 2.1G; FIBRE: 2.9G**

Ingredients:

- 250g puff pastry, fresh
- 3 tablespoons tomato sauce
- 50g ham slices
- 50g cheese slices
- 1 teaspoon dried oregano

Instructions:

Step 1: Roll out the puff pastry on a lightly floured working surface.
Step 2: Spread the tomato sauce and arrange the ham and cheese slices on top of the puff pastry.
Step 3: Sprinkle the dried oregano and roll the whole pastry into a roulade.
Step 4: Cut 1 cm slices and arrange them in an air fryer basket you sprayed with cooking spray. This is to prevent the pizza rolls from sticking.
Step 5: Cook at 180° degrees for about 15-20 minutes, checking halfway through.
Step 6: You might do this in two batches, ensuring they won't stick to each other when cooking.

TORTILLA TOAST

I just love how this toast with tortilla works. It's a sandwich, toast, and quesadilla in one. It's perfect for breakfast, brunch, or dinner. The whole family will enjoy its flavour.

- PREPARATION TIME: **10 MINUTES** | COOKING TIME: **15 MINUTES**
- SERVING SIZE: **2** | PER SERVING: **KCAL: 410; FAT: 23.1G; CARBS: 26.2G; PROTEIN: 23.7G; SUGARS: 1.9G; FIBRE: 1.3G**

Ingredients:

- 2 flour tortillas, 18 cm in diameter (or as big as your air fryer basket)
- 4 slices of cheese
- 2 tablespoons tomato sauce
- 50g marinated mushrooms
- 50g prosciutto
- 5 basil leaves
- Ground black pepper to taste

Instructions:

Step 1: Take one tortilla and spread it with tomato sauce.
Step 2: Cut the tortilla with sharp knife from the centre to one of the corners.
Step 3: On a cutting board, dice the basil leaves finely. Chop the marinated mushrooms as well.
Step 4: Arrange the cheese slices, prosciutto slices, diced mushrooms, and basil leaves. Season with ground black pepper and fold the tortilla in quarters. Repeat the same thing with the other tortilla.
Step 5: Place the tortilla toasts in the air fryer basket and air fry for about 7 minutes at 180°C. Serve and enjoy with your favourite sauce.

CINNAMON ROLLS

Who doesn't love a freshly baked cinnamon roll? They taste just like you've made them from scratch. This quick recipe will help you make a large batch of these pastries for the whole family.

- PREPARATION TIME: **10 MINUTES** | COOKING TIME: **20 MINUTES**
- SERVING SIZE: **2 PEOPLE** | PER SERVING: **KCAL: 737; FAT: 43.8G; CARBS: 79.3G; PROTEIN: 8.4G; SUGARS: 24.4G; FIBRE: 5.5G**

Ingredients:

- 250g pizza dough, fresh
- 3 tablespoons cream cheese, softened
- 4 tablespoons granulated sugar
- 2 teaspoons ground cinnamon
- ½ teaspoon vanilla extract

Instructions:

Step 1: Roll out the pizza dough on a lightly floured surface.
Step 2: Mix the cream cheese and vanilla extract in a bowl and spread on top of the rolled dough.
Step 3: Mix the granulated sugar and ground cinnamon in another bowl and sprinkle on the cream cheese.
Step 4: Roll out the whole dough into a roulade and cut 1 cm slices. This is to prevent the cinnamon rolls from sticking. Arrange them in an air fryer basket you sprayed with cooking spray.
Step 5: Cook at 180°C for about 15-20 minutes, checking after 12 minutes.
Step 6: You might do this in two batches, ensuring they won't stick to each other when cooking.

STUFFED PEPPERS

You will love this breakfast idea because it's delicious, quick to put together, and wholesome. It will keep you full until lunch, and you can make this with any kind of pepper, not only bell peppers.

PREPARATION TIME: 10 MINUTES | **COOKING TIME: 20 MINUTES**

SERVING SIZE: 2 PEOPLE | **PER SERVING: KCAL: 729; FAT: 54.1G; CARBS: 16G; PROTEIN: 44.9G; SUGARS: 9.3G; FIBRE: 2.8G**

Ingredients:

- 2 bell peppers, halved and seeds removed
- 200g breakfast sausages
- 1 onion, diced
- 1 garlic clove, minced
- 4 medium eggs, room temperature
- 100g grated cheese
- Salt and pepper to taste

Instructions:

Step 1: First, in a nonstick frying pan over medium heat, brown the breakfast sausage, and crumble it into fine pieces. This should take 5 minutes.

Step 2: Stir in the diced onion and minced garlic and season with salt and pepper to taste.

Step 3: Divide the prepared sausage mixture into the pepper halves and crack one egg in each pepper half. Sprinkle some grated cheese on top.

Step 4: Place the peppers in an air fryer basket and cook at 160°C for about 15 minutes.

Step 5: Serve and enjoy while still warm.

HOT DOGS

Making hot dogs in an air fryer won't take much time. They will become perfectly cooked, and you can place them in a hot dog bun and serve them with a hard-boiled egg or scrambled eggs, mustard, and ketchup.

PREPARATION TIME: 5 MINUTES | **COOKING TIME: 10 MINUTES**

SERVING SIZE: 2 PEOPLE | **PER SERVING: KCAL: 379; FAT: 34G; CARBS: 4.6G; PROTEIN: 12.8G; SUGARS: 3.9G; FIBRE: 0G**

Ingredients:

- 4 hot dogs
- Cooking spray

Instructions:

Step 1: Place the hot dogs in your air fryer basket. Make sure they won't stick together. This will ensure even cooking.

Step 2: Mist with cooking spray for more even browning and a perfectly golden-brown color.

Step 3: Cook for about 8-10 minutes at 160°C.

Step 4: Serve with hard-boiled egg, ketchup, mustard, and toasted buns.

BREAKFAST EGG TARTS

These breakfast tarts are made with fresh puff pastry and will become one of the best breakfast recipes you have ever tried. Easy to put together, you will enjoy these pastries with the whole family.

PREPARATION TIME: **10 MINUTES** | COOKING TIME: **20 MINUTES**

SERVING SIZE: **2 PEOPLE** | PER SERVING: **KCAL: 918; FAT: 64.8G; CARBS: 57.9G; PROTEIN: 26.5G; SUGARS: 1.8G; FIBRE: 2.2G**

Ingredients:
- 250g puff pastry, fresh
- 4 medium eggs
- Salt and pepper to taste
- 50g grated cheese
- 1 teaspoon dried oregano

Instructions:
Step 1: Roll out the puff pastry on a lightly floured working surface and cut it into 4 squares.
Step 2: Score the ends of each square with the help of a knife, being careful not to cut all the way through.
Step 3: Spray your air fryer basket with a little cooking spray and place the puff pastry squares. Crack one egg in the centre and season with salt and pepper to taste.
Step 4: Cook at 180°C for about 15 minutes.
Step 5: Sprinkle with grated cheese and dried oregano and continue cooking for 5 more minutes. Serve and enjoy.

CRISPY EGG CUPS

These egg cups are delicious and filled with ham, cheese, and some diced peppers. They make a perfect addition to any celebration, breakfast, or just a back-to-school idea for your kids.

PREPARATION TIME: **10 MINUTES** | COOKING TIME: **15 MINUTES**

SERVING SIZE: **6** | PER SERVING: **KCAL: 274; FAT: 15.6G; CARBS: 15.4G; PROTEIN: 17.9G; SUGARS: 2.3G; FIBRE: 3G**

Ingredients:
- 6 slices of toast bread
- 150g cooked ham
- 100g grated cheese
- 1 green pepper, diced into small cubes
- 5 large eggs, room temperature
- 3 tablespoons double cream
- Salt and pepper to taste

Instructions:
Step 1: First, brush 6 ramekins or silicon muffin moulds with little oil and place each piece of toast bread in it.
Step 2: Dice the ham into small cubes and set aside.
Step 3: In a large mixing bowl, mix the eggs with double cream and season with salt and pepper to taste. Stir in the grated cheese and diced ham.
Step 4: Finally, dice the green pepper into small cubes and add them to the egg mixture.
Step 5: Pour some of the egg mixture into the prepared moulds and place them into an air fryer basket.
Step 6: Cook at 170°C for about 12-15 minutes. Serve and enjoy.

SWEET CROISSANTS

Just like in Italy and France, treat yourself to a sweet homemade croissant filled with Nutella. Just before serving, dust with icing sugar for even more scrumptious presentations.

PREPARATION TIME: 15 MINUTES | **COOKING TIME: 20 MINUTES**
SERVING SIZE: 4 PEOPLE | **PER SERVING: KCAL: 633; FAT: 39.8G; CARBS: 60G; PROTEIN: 8.7G; SUGARS: 28.2G; FIBRE: 3.6G**

Ingredients:
- 250g puff pastry, fresh
- 200g Nutella
- 1 medium egg, lightly whisked
- Icing sugar, for serving

Instructions:
Step 1: First, roll out the puff pastry on a lightly floured working surface.
Step 2: Cut triangles and top 1 teaspoon to the widest part.
Step 3: Roll each piece into a crescent shape and place them in an air fryer basket.
Step 4: Brush them carefully with lightly whisked egg and cook for about 17-20 minutes at 180 C degrees. Make sure the croissants won't stick to each other for better baking.
Step 5: Just right before serving, dust with icing sugar.

PEANUT BUTTER AND JELLY FRENCH ROAST

Make a rich and decadent French toast with one of the greatest flavour combinations - peanut butter and jelly. Choose any bread and spread peanut butter while the toast is still warm.

PREPARATION TIME: 10 MINUTES | **COOKING TIME: 15 MINUTES**
SERVING SIZE: 3-4 PEOPLE | **PER SERVING: KCAL: 312; FAT: 9.2G; CARBS: 47.5G; PROTEIN: 9.1G; SUGARS: 6.9G; FIBRE: 0G**

Ingredients:
- 8 slices of brioche bread
- 2 large eggs, room temperature
- 1 teaspoon vanilla extract
- 2 tablespoons granulated sugar
- Pinch of ground cinnamon
- 3 tablespoons whole milk
- Peanut butter and jelly, for serving

Instructions:
Step 1: First, in a large mixing bowl, whisk the eggs with the vanilla, granulated sugar, cinnamon, and whole milk.
Step 2: Dip each piece of bread into the egg and milk mixture and place two to three slices of bread at a time in an air fryer basket.
Step 3: Cook at 160°C for about 10-12 minutes. Flip on the other side and cook for 5 minutes more.
Step 4: Brush the French toast with peanut butter and jelly.

HOT DOGS WITH PUFF PASTRY

For this recipe, you will need only 100g of fresh puff pastry to make a thin layer around the hot dogs. You will love this recipe because this not only looks amazing and elegant, but also is delicious and fun for kids.

PREPARATION TIME: **10 MINUTES** | COOKING TIME: **15 MINUTES**

SERVING SIZE: **2 PEOPLE** | PER SERVING: **KCAL: 866; FAT: 71.2G; CARBS: 31.5G; PROTEIN: 24.3G; SUGARS: 6.6G; FIBRE: 1.6G**

Ingredients:
- 6 hot dogs
- 1 tablespoon mustard
- 100g fresh puff pastry

Instructions:
Step 1: Roll out the puff pastry and spread the mustard over the dough.
Step 2: With the help of a knife, cut 6 long stripes 0.3 cm thick.
Step 3: Wrap the puff pastry stripes all over the hot dogs and place them in an air fryer basket, leaving space between them.
Step 4: Cook for about 12-15 minutes at 160ºC. Serve and enjoy.

SHAKSHUKA

If you love some Eastern-inspired breakfast ideas that can be made in an air fryer, then you should give this shakshuka a try. It's yummy and delicious, and the combination of tomatoes, sausages, and eggs will absolutely become your instant favourite.

PREPARATION TIME: **10 MINUTES** | COOKING TIME: **20 MINUTES**

SERVING SIZE: **2** | PER SERVING: **KCAL: 216; FAT: 14.5G; CARBS: 7.6G; PROTEIN: 13G; SUGARS: 4.8G; FIBRE: 1.4G**

Ingredients:
- 400g can of diced tomatoes
- Salt and pepper to taste
- 1 teaspoon butter
- 2 sausages
- 2 large eggs, room temperature

Instructions:
Step 1: First, grease with butter a casserole round pan that will fit into your air fryer basket.
Step 2: Dice your sausages into circles and place them in the pan with diced tomatoes.
Step 3: Season with salt and pepper to taste and cook in an air fryer for about 15 minutes at 160ºC.
Step 4: Remove from the air fryer and make two incisions with a tablespoon making space to crack in the eggs. Crack the eggs into the holes and turn the basket back in the air fryer.
Step 5: Cook at the same temperature for 5 more minutes. Serve and enjoy while still warm.

EGG CUPS

You don't know what to put in your eggs for breakfast? Make these egg cups in ramekins or silicon moulds and dump your favourite ingredients. I like to put bacon, cheese, and some chilli pepper for a little spicy flavour.

PREPARATION TIME: 7-8 MINUTES | **COOKING TIME: 15 MINUTES**

SERVING SIZE: 4 | **PER SERVING: KCAL: 245; FAT: 19G; CARBS: 1.2G; PROTEIN: 17.2G; SUGARS: 1G; FIBRE: 0.1G**

Ingredients:
- 2 teaspoons butter
- 4 large eggs, room temperature
- 100g gouda cheese
- 1 red chilli pepper
- 50g bacon
- Salt and pepper to taste

Instructions:
Step 1: First, in a large mixing bowl, crack in the eggs and whisk them with salt and pepper to taste.
Step 2: With the help of your kitchen grater, grate the cheese and stir it into the egg mixture.
Step 3: On a wooden board, dice the chilli pepper into smaller pieces alongside the bacon and stir them into the egg mixture.
Step 4: Brush four ramekins with butter and pour the egg mixture. Bake for about 12-15 minutes at 170°C. Serve and enjoy.

BACON-WRAPPED HARD-BOILED EGGS

These bacon wrapped hard-boiled eggs are delicious and always a creative way to your guests.

PREPARATION TIME: 10 MINUTES | **COOKING TIME: 8 MINUTES**

SERVING SIZE: 4 | **PER SERVING: KCAL: 182; FAT: 13.4G; CARBS: 1.3G; PROTEIN: 13.7G; SUGARS: 0.5G; FIBRE: 0.3G**

Ingredients:
- 4 large eggs, room temperature
- 2 teaspoons mustard
- 4 slices of bacon
- Pepper to taste

Instructions:
Step 1: First, wash the eggs and clean them with kitchen paper.
Step 2: Place them in an air fryer basket and cook for about 5-7 minutes at 200°C.
Step 3: Let them steep in cold water for 5 minutes and peel them thoroughly.
Step 4: Carefully brush them with mustard and wrap them in bacon.
Step 5: Place the wrapped hard-boiled eggs in the air fryer basket again and cook for 5 more minutes at 180°C. Serve with mustard and ketchup and a toasted bun.

HARD-BOILED EGGS

Did you know that you can perfect hard-boiled eggs in an air fryer? They will only take around 5-6 minutes at 200°C, and they are perfectly cooked for everyone's taste. You can serve them with your favourite hollandaise sauce or hot dogs.

PREPARATION TIME: **2 MINUTES** | COOKING TIME: **5-6 MINUTES**

SERVING SIZE: **6 HARD-BOILED EGGS** | PER SERVING: **KCAL: 111; FAT: 7.5G; CARBS: 3.3G; PROTEIN: 7.7G; SUGARS: 0.6G; FIBRE: 0.1G**

Ingredients:
- 6 large eggs, room temperature
- Hollandaise sauce, for serving
- Hot dogs, for serving
- Mustard and ketchup if desired for serving

Instructions:
Step 1: First wash your eggs with lukewarm water and clean them with a paper towel.
Step 2: Arrange them in an air fryer basket, being careful not to overcrowd the air fryer basket.
Step 3: Cook for about 5-6 minutes at 200°C.
Step 4: Dip them in cold water and let them steep for 5 minutes.
Step 5: Crack each egg, peel the shell and serve with hot dogs, hollandaise sauce, and mustard or ketchup if desired.

EGGS AND SAUSAGES

If you love some delicious sausages and eggs for breakfast, then this is the recipe you need to try. It's delicious and always so easy to put together.

PREPARATION TIME: **10 MINUTES** | COOKING TIME: **20 MINUTES**

SERVING SIZE: **2** | PER SERVING: **KCAL: 455; FAT: 36.1G; CARBS: 2G; PROTEIN: 30.5G; SUGARS: 1.2G; FIBRE: 0.2G**

Ingredients:
- 2 sausages
- 4 large eggs, room temperature
- 100g grated cheese
- Salt and pepper to taste
- 1 teaspoon butter
- 1 spring onion, for serving

Instructions:
Step 1: First, dice the sausages into smaller pieces (circles or cubes).
Step 2: Grate your cheese with a kitchen grater.
Step 3: In a large mixing bowl, crack in the eggs and season with salt and pepper to taste.
Step 4: Grease a nonstick casserole pan that can fit into an air fryer basket with butter and add in the diced sausages.
Step 5: Cook for about 5 minutes at 170°C.
Step 6: Remove from the air fryer and stir in the whisked eggs. Cook for about 7 minutes at 170°C
Step 7: Finally, stir until everything is combined and sprinkle grated cheese on top.
Step 8: To serve, slice the spring onion into smaller pieces and sprinkle on top. Enjoy.

BREAKFAST PIZZA

I think this will become your kid's favourite. I mean, who doesn't love a nice slice of pizza any time of the day? You will love this fantastic breakfast pizza that's made with the crescent dough in a blink of an eye.

- **PREPARATION TIME:** 10 MINUTES | **COOKING TIME:** 15 MINUTES
- **SERVING SIZE:** 2 | **PER SERVING:** KCAL: 608; FAT: 34.9G; CARBS: 50.7G; PROTEIN: 18.2G; SUGARS: 14.1G; FIBRE: 0.4G

Ingredients:
- 250g crescent dough
- 2 tablespoons tomato sauce
- 100g mozzarella cheese
- 50g pepperoni slices
- ½ teaspoon dried oregano

Instructions:
Step 1: First, roll out the crescent dough on a piece of parchment paper the size that will fit into your air fryer.

Step 2: With a kitchen grated grate, your mozzarella cheese and set aside.

Step 3: Cook for about 5 minutes at 180°C. Remove from the air fryer and spread with tomato sauce, pepperoni slices, and grated mozzarella cheese.

Step 4: Sprinkle with dried oregano and cook for about 10-12 minutes more at 170°C.

Step 5: Serve while still warm and enjoy.

BREAKFAST TORTILLA

Add your favourite sandwich toppings and fold them into your tortilla. Air fry for about 5-7 minutes for a crispy outside and melty, cheesy inside. Yum!

- **PREPARATION TIME:** 10 MINUTES | **COOKING TIME:** 15 MINUTES
- **SERVING SIZE:** 2 | **PER SERVING:** KCAL: 521; FAT: 35.2G; CARBS: 25.3G; PROTEIN: 24G; SUGARS: 1.3G; FIBRE: 1G

Ingredients:
- 2 flour tortillas 18 cm in diameter (or as your air fryer basket)
- 4 slices of cheese
- 50g pepperoni slices
- 2 tablespoons cream cheese
- Salt and pepper to taste
- 50g marinated mushrooms

Instructions:
Step 1: Take each of your tortillas and spread them with cream cheese.

Step 2: Arrange cheese and pepperoni slices and season with salt and pepper to taste.

Step 3: Dice your marinated mushrooms into fine pieces and arrange them into your tortillas.

Step 4: Fold in half, being careful not to overcrowd the tortillas.

Step 5: Cook for about 5-7 minutes at 160°C and serve with your favourite sauce.

PUFF PASTRY MINI PIES

With fresh puff pastry, a little cheese, some diced anchovies, and a drizzle of olive oil for extra flavour, these mini pies with puff pastry are delicious to start your day off.

PREPARATION TIME: **10 MINUTES** | COOKING TIME: **15 MINUTES**
SERVING SIZE: **4** | PER SERVING: **KCAL: 509; FAT: 34.4G; CARBS: 31.1G; PROTEIN: 19G; SUGARS: 2.7G; FIBRE: 1.2G**

Ingredients:

- 250g puff pastry, fresh
- 2 tablespoons chopped anchovies
- 100g cheese
- 4 tablespoons Greek yoghurt
- 1 teaspoon mustard
- ½ teaspoon dried dill
- Salt and pepper to taste
- ½ teaspoon dried oregano
- 1 tablespoon parsley

Instructions:

Step 1: First, chop your parsley into fine pieces.
Step 2: With the help of your kitchen grater, grate the cheese and set aside.
Step 3: In a bowl, whisk the Greek yoghurt, dried dill, salt, and pepper to taste, chopped parsley, mustard, and chopped anchovies.
Step 4: Roll out the puff pastry on a lightly floured working surface and cut squares.
Step 5: Add a dollop of the Greek yoghurt mixture in the centre of each piece of puff pastry and place one or two pieces of pastry in an air fryer basket lined with a piece of parchment paper.
Step 6: Top with some grated cheese and cook for 15 minutes at 180°C.
Step 7: Repeat the same process until you cook all the pastries. Serve and enjoy.

STUFFED AVOCADO

Transform your avocado into a boat filled with soft-baked eggs, perfectly seasoned and ready to be enjoyed for breakfast. You will enjoy every bite, dipping your slice of bread into the medium-cooked egg. Yum!

PREPARATION TIME: **5 MINUTES** | COOKING TIME: **10 MINUTES**
SERVING SIZE: **1 PERSON** | PER SERVING: **KCAL: 543; FAT: 46.9G; CARBS: 23.1G; PROTEIN: 14G; SUGARS: 2.2G; FIBRE: 14G**

Ingredients:

- 1 avocado, ripe
- 2 small eggs, room temperature
- Salt and pepper to taste
- 1 chilli pepper, diced thinly
- 1 tablespoon parsley, chopped finely
- 1 slice of bread for serving

Instructions:

Step 1: Cut the avocado in half and remove the pit.
Step 2: Season with salt and pepper to taste and place the avocados in the air fryer basket.
Step 3: Crack the eggs in each avocado hole and cook at 160°C for about 10-12 minutes.
Step 4: Add some sliced chilli on top and cook for 1 more minute.
Step 5: Serve with a sprinkle of parsley and a slice of bread. Enjoy.

Please scan the QR code below to access your bonus PDF with all 150 recipes with full coloured photos & beautiful designs alongside!

This is the only way we can get the recipes with coloured photos to you & keep the book as reasonably priced as possible.

Also, once downloaded you can take the PDF with you digitally wherever you go- meaning you can cook these recipes wherever you may be! (As long as you have an air fryer!)

We hope you enjoy and do let us know your feedback!

STEP BY STEP GUIDE TO ACCESS

1. Open Your Phones (Or Any Device You Want The Book On) Back Camera. The Back Camera Is The One You use as if you are taking a picture of someone.
2. Simply point your Camera at the QR code and 'tap' the QR code with your finger to focus the camera.
3. A link / pop up will appear. Simply tap that (and make sure you have internet connection) and the FREE PDF containing all of the coloured images should appear.
4. Now you have access to these FOREVER. Simply 'Bookmark' The tab it opened on, or download the document and take wherever you want.
5. Repeat this on any device you want it on! (If you want it on a laptop, simply email the document to yourself!)

SNACK / APPETIZER *Recipes*

— 30 RECIPES —

TORTILLA CHIPS

Do you want to make homemade tortilla chips in almost no time? You just need to toss your diced tortilla with some salt and olive oil, dump it in an air fryer, and cook for 7-8 minutes until perfection.

PREPARATION TIME: 5 MINUTES | **COOKING TIME: 7-8 MINUTES**

SERVING SIZE: 2 PEOPLE | **PER SERVING: KCAL: 125; FAT: 3.7G; CARBS: 24.1G; PROTEIN: 2.7G; SUGARS: 0.4G; FIBRE: 3G**

Ingredients:
- 4 flour tortillas
- 1 teaspoon olive oil
- Salt to taste

Instructions:
Step 1: First, on a wooden board, place your tortillas and cut them in half. Then, each half is cut in quarters and each quarter in half.

Step 2: Take each piece of diced tortilla and dice it into small triangles so you can get around 4 triangle pieces from each of the diced tortillas.

Step 3: Place the tortilla triangles into a large mixing bowl and drizzle the olive oil and salt to taste.

Step 4: Toss everything well with your hands and transfer the tortilla chips into an air fryer basket.

Step 5: Cook for about 7-8 minutes at 180°C and serve to enjoy with your favourite salsa or dipping sauce.

STUFFED MUSHROOMS

Stuffed mushrooms are perfect for the days you want to show off in front of your family and friends. This recipe is absolutely amazing, easy to put together, and as tasty as it looks.

PREPARATION TIME: 15 MINUTES | **COOKING TIME: 10 MINUTES**

SERVING SIZE: 2 PEOPLE | **PER SERVING: KCAL: 292; FAT: 21.2G; CARBS: 6.5G; PROTEIN: 20.4G; SUGARS: 3.2G; FIBRE: 1.5G**

Ingredients:
- 250g white button mushrooms
- 1 teaspoon onion powder
- Salt and pepper to taste
- 50g bacon
- 50g gouda cheese
- 2 tablespoons cream cheese
- 2 tablespoons fresh parsley

Instructions:
Step 1: First, remove the stems of the mushrooms and dice them finely.

Step 2: Place the diced stems in a bowl and stir in the onion powder, salt, and pepper to taste, and the cream cheese.

Step 3: Dice the bacon into small pieces and stir them into the bowl with diced mushrooms.

Step 4: Stuff the mushrooms with the creamy mixture and arrange the stuffed mushrooms in an air fryer basket.

Step 5: Top with grated cheese and cook for about 10 minutes at 170°C.

Step 6: Finely dice the parsley and sprinkle over cooked stuffed mushrooms. Enjoy.

MOZZARELLA STICKS

Make these mozzarella sticks from scratch and enjoy excellent party food with your friends and family. They make a perfect appetizer for your upcoming guests or whenever you want to snack on something in front of the TV.

PREPARATION TIME: 15 MINUTES | **COOKING TIME: 7-8 MINUTES**
SERVING SIZE: 2 PEOPLE | **PER SERVING: KCAL: 622; FAT: 27G; CARBS: 64.7G; PROTEIN: 29.2G; SUGARS: 1.8G; FIBRE: 5.2G**

Ingredients:

- 250g mozzarella sticks, frozen
- 50g all-purpose flour
- Salt and pepper to taste
- 1 large egg
- 50g breadcrumbs

Instructions:

Step 1: First, Place the flour in one plate and set aside.
Step 2: Mix the breadcrumbs with salt and pepper to taste and set them aside on a plate.
Step 3: Whisk the egg lightly with the help of a fork.
Step 4: Cover each of the mozzarella sticks in flour and then dip them in the whisked egg.
Step 5: Finally, coat them with breadcrumbs.
Step 6: Spray your air fryer basket with a little bit of cooking spray and arrange the mozzarella sticks, being careful not to touch each other.
Step 7: Cook for about 7 minutes at 150°C. Serve and enjoy.

CAULIFLOWER STEAKS

If you are vegan or love to eat healthy food, then these cauliflower steaks are everything you need to try this cauliflower season. The seasoned slice of cauliflower will be perfect with a drizzle of your favourite sauce.

PREPARATION TIME: 5 MINUTES | **COOKING TIME: 20 MINUTES**
SERVING SIZE: 2 PEOPLE | **PER SERVING: KCAL: 109; FAT: 7.9G; CARBS: 9.4G; PROTEIN: 3G; SUGARS: 4.2G; FIBRE: 3.5G**

Ingredients:

- 1 cauliflower head, large
- Salt and pepper to taste
- 1 tablespoon olive oil
- 1 teaspoon chilli flakes
- 1 teaspoon Italian seasoning
- 1 teaspoon onion powder
- 1 teaspoon garlic powder
- 1 teaspoon paprika powder

Instructions:

Step 1: First, wash and clean the cauliflower head and dice into 1 cm thick steak slices.
Step 2: Brush with a little bit of olive oil and set them aside.
Step 3: In a medium-sized mixing bowl, mix the chilli flakes, salt, and pepper to taste, Italian seasoning, onion powder, garlic powder, and paprika powder.
Step 4: Sprinkle the brushed cauliflower steaks with the seasonings and place them in an air fryer basket – one or two at a time, so they will cook perfectly.
Step 5: Cook for about 20 minutes at 180°C.
Step 6: Serve with your favourite sauce and enjoy.

STUFFED JALAPENOS

If you'd like something delicious and perfect for entertaining, this is a recipe for you. The spicy jalapenos wrapped in bacon make a quick appetizer that will leave your guests speechless.

PREPARATION TIME: 15 MINUTES | **COOKING TIME: 10 MINUTES**

SERVING SIZE: 2 PEOPLE | **PER SERVING: KCAL: 246; FAT: 14.8G; CARBS: 8.3G; PROTEIN: 20.1G; SUGARS: 3G; FIBRE: 3.3G**

Ingredients:

- 250g jalapeno peppers
- 100g cottage cheese
- 1 medium egg
- Salt and pepper to taste
- 50g bacon stripes

Instructions:

Step 1: First, cut the jalapeno peppers in half lengthwise, then remove the seeds and stems.

Step 2: In a large mixing bowl, mix the cottage cheese with the egg and season with salt and pepper to taste.

Step 3: Stuff the jalapeno peppers with the cottage cheese mixture and wrap each pepper in bacon.

Step 4: Cook the bacon-wrapped jalapeno peppers in an air fryer at 170°C for about 8-10 minutes. Serve and enjoy.

COURGETTE FRIES

If you like a snack that goes perfectly fine with your glass of beer, you will love these courgette fries. They are quick to make and delicious in every bite.

PREPARATION TIME: 10 MINUTES | **COOKING TIME: 17-20 MINUTES**

SERVING SIZE: 2 PEOPLE | **PER SERVING: KCAL: 334; FAT: 7.5G; CARBS: 51.8; PROTEIN: 15.8G; SUGARS: 6.9G; FIBRE: 7.5G**

Ingredients:

- 2 medium sized courgettes
- Salt to taste
- 2 medium eggs
- 100g breadcrumbs
- 3 tablespoons all-purpose flour

Instructions:

Step 1: First, cut the courgettes into strips that are 6-7 cm long and ½ cm wide.

Step 2: Season them with salt and let them steep for about 10 minutes to release the moisture.

Step 3: Drain well and tap them with kitchen paper.

Step 4: Crack the egg in a bowl and whisk with the help of a fork.

Step 5: Sprinkle flour over the courgette fries and then dip them in the lightly whisked egg.

Step 6: Finally, coat them with breadcrumbs and arrange them in an air fryer basket, careful not to touch each other.

Step 7: Spray them a little with cooking spray and cook for about 15 minutes at 170°C. Check them halfway through and serve them to enjoy with your favourite dipping sauce.

COURGETTE PANCAKES

These courgette pancakes are so good that you will love them not only as a snack but for breakfast, brunch, or even dinner. With a dollop of Greek Yoghurt, this is a delicious and absolutely amazing appetizer with a dollop of Greek yoghurt.

PREPARATION TIME: 10 MINUTES | **COOKING TIME: 17-20 MINUTES**
SERVING SIZE: 2 PEOPLE | **PER SERVING:** KCAL: 116; FAT: 2.8G; CARBS: 18.1G; PROTEIN: 6.1G; SUGARS: 4G; FIBRE: 2.4G

Ingredients:

- 1 medium courgette
- 1 large egg, room temperature,
- 1 teaspoon baking powder
- Salt and pepper to taste
- 1 carrot
- 1 teaspoon onion powder
- ½ teaspoon garlic powder
- 3 tablespoons all-purpose flour

Instructions:

Step 1: First, wash and clean the courgette and grate on your kitchen grater. Squeeze out the liquid and place the grated courgette in a clean bowl.
Step 2: Peel and grate the carrot and place it in the bowl with the courgette.
Step 3: Crack in the egg and season with salt and pepper to taste, onion powder, and garlic powder.
Step 4: Add in the baking powder and all-purpose flour and stir until just combined.
Step 5: Line your air fryer basket with a piece of parchment paper and spray it with cooking spray.
Step 6: Add 2-3 tablespoons of the courgette batter and cook for about 7 minutes at 180°C.
Step 7: Flip the courgette pancake on the other side and cook for about 5 more minutes at 180°C.
Step 8: Serve with Greek yoghurt and enjoy.

CRISPY RAVIOLI

This recipe is my favourite appetizer or party food because it can be prepared in almost no time. You will love every bite of this yummy party food.

PREPARATION TIME: 5 MINUTES | **COOKING TIME: 10 MINUTES**
SERVING SIZE: 2 PEOPLE | **PER SERVING:** KCAL: 733; FAT: 43.3G; CARBS: 38.5G; PROTEIN: 24.4G; SUGARS: 21G; FIBRE: 9.3G

Ingredients:

- 300g ravioli, with cheese, spinach, or mushroom filling
- 1 tablespoon olive oil
- 30g parmesan cheese
- 1 teaspoon dried oregano

Instructions:

Step 1: First, bring pot with salted water to a boil.
Step 2: Cook the ravioli for 2-3 minutes less than the package instruction says.
Step 3: Drain the raviolis well and place them in a large mixing bowl.
Step 4: Stir in the olive oil. grated parmesan cheese, and dried oregano.
Step 5: Mix and toss everything together and transfer the mixture into an air fryer basket.
Step 6: Cook for about 10 minutes until crispy and lightly golden brown in color.
Step 7: Serve with tomato sauce for dipping sauce.

ROASTED CAULIFLOWER

If you love cauliflower, then you will enjoy this amazing recipe. It's seasoned perfectly and the time won't take you more than 20 minutes to make. This is a recipe that you want to make over and over when you want a healthy snack idea.

PREPARATION TIME: 5 MINUTES | **COOKING TIME: 20 MINUTES**

SERVING SIZE: 2 PEOPLE | **PER SERVING: KCAL: 108; FAT: 7.4G; CARBS: 10.2G; PROTEIN: 3.2G; SUGARS: 4.1G; FIBRE: 4.3G**

Ingredients:

- 1 cauliflower head, medium-sized
- Salt and pepper to taste
- 1 tablespoon olive oil
- 1 teaspoon chilli flakes
- 1 teaspoon dried oregano
- 1 teaspoon onion powder
- 1 teaspoon garlic powder
- 1 teaspoon smoked paprika
- 1 teaspoon apple cider vinegar

Instructions:

Step 1: First, wash and clean the cauliflower head and dice into small florets.
Step 2: Place the cauliflower florets in a bowl and season with salt and pepper to taste, olive oil, chilli flakes, dried oregano, onion powder, garlic powder, smoked paprika, and apple cider vinegar.
Step 3: Toss everything together until fully mixed and combined and transfer it into an air fryer basket.
Step 4: Cook at 180°C for about 15-20 minutes.
Step 5: After 15 minutes, check if they need to cook for 5 more minutes so they develop a nice golden-brown color on top.
Step 6: Serve with your favourite dipping sauce.

SPICY TOFU

Did you know that you can make perfectly cooked tofu in an air fryer? This will be one of the best appetizers or side dishes ever.

PREPARATION TIME: 5 MINUTES | **COOKING TIME: 15 MINUTES**

SERVING SIZE: 2 PEOPLE | **PER SERVING: KCAL: 198; FAT: 13.3G; CARBS: 9.2G; PROTEIN: 13.6G; SUGARS: 1.1G; FIBRE: 1.6G**

Ingredients:

- 300g tofu, drained
- Salt and pepper to taste
- 1 teaspoon hot paprika powder
- 2 tablespoons all-purpose flour
- 1 tablespoon soya sauce
- 1 teaspoon apple cider vinegar
- 1 tablespoon olive oil

Instructions:

Step 1: First, drain your tofu well and place it in a bowl.
Step 2: Season with salt and pepper to taste, soya sauce, hot paprika powder, and apple cider vinegar.
Step 3: Sprinkle all-purpose flour and coat each side of each piece of tofu well.
Step 4: Arrange the tofu slices in an air fryer basket and drizzle them with olive oil.
Step 5: Cook for about 15 minutes at 180°C.
Step 6: After 10 minutes, remove the air fryer basket and shake it slightly to prevent your tofu slices from sticking.
Step 7: Serve and enjoy over a bowl with cooked rice.

CAULIFLOWER CAKES

For brunch or just for snacking with your family or friends, these cauliflower cakes are perfect for everyone's taste.

PREPARATION TIME: **5 MINUTES** | COOKING TIME: **20 MINUTES**

 SERVING SIZE: **2 PEOPLE** | PER SERVING: **KCAL: 324; FAT: 13G; CARBS: 39.9G; PROTEIN: 13.9G; SUGARS: 5.1G; FIBRE: 4.9G**

Ingredients:
- 1 cauliflower head, medium
- Salt and pepper to taste
- 1 tablespoon olive oil
- 1 teaspoon chilli flakes
- 1 teaspoon Herbs de Provence
- 1 teaspoon onion powder
- 1 teaspoon garlic powder
- 2 large eggs, room temperature
- 60g all-purpose flour
- 3 tablespoons breadcrumbs
- 2 tablespoons parsley, chopped

Instructions:
Step 1: First, wash and clean the cauliflower head and grate on your kitchen grater finely.
Step 2: Season with salt and pepper to taste, olive oil, chilli flakes, Herbs de Provence, onion powder, and garlic powder.
Step 3: Crack in the eggs, flour, breadcrumbs, and chopped parsley and mix until everything is combined.
Step 4: Form small patties from the mixture and arrange several in the air fryer basket.
Step 5: Spray with a little bit of cooking spray and cook for about 15-20 minutes at 180°C.
Step 6: After 10 minutes, flip them on the other side for even more cooking. Serve and enjoy with some sauce of your choice.

....

AUBERGINE FRIES

This simple and easy recipe will become one of your favourite snacks.

PREPARATION TIME: **5 MINUTES** | COOKING TIME: **15-18 MINUTES**

 SERVING SIZE: **2 PEOPLE** | PER SERVING: **KCAL: 120; FAT: 7.5G; CARBS: 14G; PROTEIN: 2.3G; SUGARS: 6.9G; FIBRE: 8.4G**

Ingredients:
- 1 large Aubergine
- Salt and pepper to taste
- 1 tablespoon olive oil
- 1 teaspoon dried oregano

Instructions:
Step 1: First, wash and clean the Aubergine and dice in 7 cm stick slices in a fry shape.
Step 2: Place the Aubergine sticks in a large mixing bowl.
Step 3: Toss with salt and pepper to taste, olive oil, and dried oregano.
Step 4: Transfer the fries in an air fryer basket and cook for about 15-20 minutes at 180°C, depending on the crispiness you prefer.
Step 5: Serve with sour cream or ranch dressing.

SPICY CAULIFLOWER FLORETS

Want something spicy and delicious at the same time? You will love these hot and delicious cauliflower florets. Perfect finger food for a family gathering in front of the TV.

PREPARATION TIME: 5 MINUTES | **COOKING TIME: 20 MINUTES**

SERVING SIZE: 2 PEOPLE | **PER SERVING: KCAL: 118; FAT: 7.2G; CARBS: 12.2G; PROTEIN: 3G; SUGARS: 7.1G; FIBRE: 3.6G**

Ingredients:

- 1 cauliflower head, medium
- Salt and pepper to taste
- 1 tablespoon olive oil
- 1 teaspoon chilli flakes
- 1 teaspoon Herbs de Provence
- 1 teaspoon onion powder
- 1 teaspoon garlic powder
- 1 tablespoon hot sauce
- 1 tablespoon sweet chilli sauce
- 1 teaspoon hot smoked paprika

Instructions:

Step 1: First, wash and clean the cauliflower head and dice into small florets.

Step 2: Sprinkle and season with salt and pepper to taste, olive oil, chilli flakes, Herbs de Provence, onion powder, garlic powder, hot sauce, sweet chilli sauce, and hot smoked paprika.

Step 3: Toss everything with the help of a spatula and transfer the cauliflower florets into an air fryer basket.

Step 4: Cook for about 20 minutes at 180°C.

Step 5: Serve with your favourite sauce and enjoy.

....

CRISPY CHEESE

This is something that I enjoy cooking and serving for my family and friends. I love cheese and these crispy bites are perfect for any kind of party.

PREPARATION TIME: 5 MINUTES | **COOKING TIME: 10 MINUTES**

SERVING SIZE: 2 PEOPLE | **PER SERVING: KCAL: 745; FAT: 47.1G; CARBS: 38.6G; PROTEIN: 51.6G; SUGARS: 2.1G; FIBRE: 1.8G**

Ingredients:

- 300g block of cheese
- 30g all-purpose flour
- 1 large egg, room temperature
- 60g breadcrumbs

Instructions:

Step 1: First, dice small cubes from the cheese block and set them aside.

Step 2: Coat each cheese cube with flour.

Step 3: Crack the egg in a bowl and whisk with the help of a fork. Coat each cheese cube in the whisked egg, and finally, coat them in breadcrumbs.

Step 4: Arrange the cheese cubes in an air fryer basket and cook for about 8-10 minutes at 170°C. Serve and enjoy while still warm.

AUBERGINE PARMIGIANA

This quick and easy appetizer idea will absolutely leave your guests speechless. You will adore how this dish is easy to put together and how tasty it is.

PREPARATION TIME: 5 MINUTES | **COOKING TIME: 15 MINUTES**

SERVING SIZE: 2 PEOPLE | **PER SERVING: KCAL: 204; FAT: 12.8G; CARBS: 15.8G; PROTEIN: 10.6G; SUGARS: 8G; FIBRE: 8.5G**

Ingredients:
- 1 large Aubergine
- Salt and pepper to taste
- 1 tablespoon olive oil
- 10 teaspoons tomato sauce
- 50g grated parmesan cheese

Instructions:
- **Step 1:** First, wash and clean the aubergine and dice into 0,5 cm thick slices.
- **Step 2:** Season them with salt and pepper to taste and drizzle just a little bit of olive oil.
- **Step 3:** Arrange the aubergine slices in an air fryer basket and cook for about 8 minutes at 180°C degrees.
- **Step 4:** Add 1 teaspoon to each piece of aubergine and sprinkle some grated parmesan cheese on top.
- **Step 5:** Continue cooking at 180°C for 5-7 minutes. Serve and enjoy as they are.

CRISPY CHICKPEAS

You will adore this fantastic snack that is ready in almost no time. Just season your chickpeas with the right seasonings and enjoy this delicious flavour.

PREPARATION TIME: 5 MINUTES | **COOKING TIME: 10 MINUTES**

SERVING SIZE: 2 PEOPLE | **PER SERVING: KCAL: 708; FAT: 18.4G; CARBS: 107.1G; PROTEIN: 34G; SUGARS: 19.1G; FIBRE: 30.9G**

Ingredients:
- 350g chickpeas, drained
- Salt and pepper to taste
- 1 teaspoon smoked paprika
- 1 teaspoon chilli flakes
- 1 teaspoon Italian seasoning
- 1 tablespoon olive oil

Instructions:
- **Step 1:** In a large mixing bowl place the chickpeas, well-drained from can or jar.
- **Step 2:** Season them with salt and pepper to taste smoked paprika, chilli flakes, and Italian seasoning.
- **Step 3:** Toss until everything is well mixed and combined.
- **Step 4:** Transfer the chickpeas to the air fryer basket and cook for about 10 minutes at 160°C. Serve and enjoy.

AUBERGINE STICKS

If you want a more rich and more delicious taste to the classic Aubergine fries, then you will adore this next recipe.

- **PREPARATION TIME: 5 MINUTES** | **COOKING TIME: 15-18 MINUTES**
- **SERVING SIZE: 2 PEOPLE** | **PER SERVING: KCAL: 153; FAT: 9.9G; CARBS: 13.7G; PROTEIN: 5.4G; SUGARS: 7.1G; FIBRE: 8.1G**

Ingredients:

- 1 large Aubergine
- Salt and pepper to taste
- 1 tablespoon olive oil
- 1 large egg, lightly whisked
- 50g Panko breadcrumbs

Instructions:

Step 1: First, wash and clean the Aubergine and dice in 7 cm fry-shaped stick slices.
Step 2: Place the Aubergine sticks in a large mixing bowl.
Step 3: Season with salt and pepper to taste and coat them with the lightly whisked egg.
Step 4: Coat them well in breadcrumbs and arrange them in an air fryer basket.
Step 5: Be careful so the sticks won't touch together.
Step 6: Spray with cooking spray or drizzle with olive oil just a little bit for an even better browning and crispier taste.
Step 7: Bake for about 15-18 minutes at 180ºC.

STICKY AND SWEET AIR FRYER AUBERGINE

An amazing dish that can be served as a snack, light dinner, or even a side dish to your next festive table.

- **PREPARATION TIME: 5 MINUTES** | **COOKING TIME: 15 MINUTES**
- **SERVING SIZE: 2 PEOPLE** | **PER SERVING: KCAL: 165; FAT: 7.6G; CARBS: 24.7G; PROTEIN: 3G; SUGARS: 17.2G; FIBRE: 8.3G**

Ingredients:

- 1 large Aubergine
- Salt and pepper to taste
- 1 tablespoon olive oil
- 1 tablespoon soya sauce
- 1 tablespoon Worcestershire sauce
- 1 teaspoon paprika powder
- 1 tablespoon honey
- 1 teaspoon cumin powder

Instructions:

Step 1: First, wash and clean the aubergine and dice into small cubes. About 1 cm each.
Step 2: Place the diced aubergine in a large mixing bowl and season with salt and pepper to taste, olive oil, soya sauce, Worcestershire sauce, paprika powder, honey, and cumin powder.
Step 3: Toss everything together until combined and transfer it to an air fryer basket.
Step 4: Cook for about 18 minutes at 170ºC and then remove the basket from the air fryer and shake everything together.
Step 5: Put the air fryer basket back and cook for 8 more minutes until crispy, golden, and shiny.
Step 6: Serve with crumbled feta on top if desired or chopped parsley.

CRISPY BRAIDED TOFU

This can be served at your next big party! Your guests will absolutely love this finger food that is delicious and crispy in every bite.

PREPARATION TIME: **5 MINUTES** | COOKING TIME: **15 MINUTES**

SERVING SIZE: **2 PEOPLE** | PER SERVING: **KCAL: 249; FAT: 11.5G; CARBS: 7.7G; PROTEIN: 16.3G; SUGARS: 1.5G; FIBRE: 1.9G**

Ingredients:
- 300g tofu, drained
- Salt and pepper to taste
- 1 teaspoon Italian seasoning
- 1 large egg, room temperature
- 50g Panko breadcrumbs
- 1 teaspoon smoked paprika

Instructions:
Step 1: First, dice the tofu into 1 cm square pieces.
Step 2: Season with salt and pepper to taste and Italian seasoning.
Step 3: Dip each piece in lightly whisked egg with the help of a fork and coat well on each side.
Step 4: In another bowl, mix the breadcrumbs and smoked paprika together until combined.
Step 5: Coat each piece of tofu into the breadcrumb mixture and arrange the pieces in an air fryer basket.
Step 6: Spray with cooking spray and cook for about 15 minutes until golden brown and crispy at 180°C degrees.
Step 7: Serve and enjoy with your favourite dipping sauce.

PASTA CHIPS

These pasta chips are crunchy snacks, perfect for entertaining your friends. This is a great party food that bursts with flavour and unique taste.

PREPARATION TIME: **5 MINUTES** | COOKING TIME: **10 MINUTES**

SERVING SIZE: **2 PEOPLE** | PER SERVING: **KCAL: 540; FAT: 13.3G; CARBS: 84.3G; PROTEIN: 21.4G; SUGARS: 1G; FIBRE: 0.7G**

Ingredients:
- 300g rigatoni pasta
- Salt and pepper to taste
- 1 tablespoon olive oil
- 25g parmesan cheese
- 3 tablespoons tomato sauce
- 1 teaspoon dried oregano

Instructions:
Step 1: First, bring pot with salted water to a boil.
Step 2: Cook the rigatoni pasta for 2-3 minutes less than the package instructions.
Step 3: Drain the pasta well and place them in a large mixing bowl.
Step 4: Stir in the olive oil and grated parmesan cheese, tomato sauce, and dried oregano.
Step 5: Mix and toss everything together and transfer the mixture into an air fryer basket.
Step 6: Cook for about 10 minutes until crispy and lightly golden brown in color.
Step 7: Serve with tomato sauce for dipping sauce.

AIR FRYER MUSHROOMS

Amazing flavour is always developed by the simplest of ingredients. You will adore this delicious snack idea, perfectly seasoned for everyone's taste.

PREPARATION TIME: 5 MINUTES | **COOKING TIME: 10 MINUTES**

SERVING SIZE: 2 PEOPLE | **PER SERVING: KCAL: 107; FAT: 7.6G; CARBS: 7.4G; PROTEIN: 6.5G; SUGARS: 3.6G; FIBRE: 2.3G**

Ingredients:
- 400g white button mushrooms
- Salt and pepper to taste
- 1 tablespoon olive oil
- ½ teaspoon garlic powder
- 1 teaspoon dried thyme

Instructions:
Step 1: In a large mixing bowl place the white button mushrooms.
Step 2: Season with salt and pepper to taste, olive oil, garlic powder, and dried thyme.
Step 3: Toss everything together until fully combined and transfer the mixture to an air fryer basket.
Step 4: Cook for about 10 minutes at 180°C.
Step 5: Serve with toothpicks as a party food and enjoy.

FRIED PICKLES

Fried pickles are always a great idea for a snack or an appetizer idea that will wow your guests.

PREPARATION TIME: 5 MINUTES | **COOKING TIME: 10 MINUTES**

SERVING SIZE: 2 PEOPLE | **PER SERVING: KCAL: 180; FAT: 5.6G; CARBS: 12.2G; PROTEIN: 6.4G; SUGARS: 3.5G; FIBRE: 4.1G**

Ingredients:
- 10 pickles, medium-sized
- 50g Panko breadcrumbs
- 1 tablespoon grated parmesan cheese
- 1 teaspoon dried dill

Instructions:
Step 1: In a large mixing bowl place the breadcrumbs and mix it with grated parmesan cheese and dried dill.
Step 2: Mix until everything is combined and set aside.
Step 3: Dice your pickles into 3 mm thick slices and coat them well with the breadcrumb mixture.
Step 4: Arrange them in the air fryer basket and cook for about 10 minutes at 170°C degrees.
Step 5: Serve with ranch dressing if desired.

BRAIDED ASPARAGUS

This is another asparagus recipe that is crispy and perfect for snacking.

PREPARATION TIME: 5 MINUTES | **COOKING TIME:** 10 MINUTES
SERVING SIZE: 2 PEOPLE | **PER SERVING:** KCAL: 249; FAT: 11.9G; CARBS: 12.4G; PROTEIN: 7.6G; SUGARS: 3.7G; FIBRE: 3.4G

Ingredients:
- 300g fresh asparagus
- Salt and pepper to taste
- 1 tablespoon olive oil
- 1 teaspoon onion powder
- ½ teaspoon garlic powder
- 1 large egg, room temperature
- 60g Panko breadcrumbs

Instructions:
Step 1: In a large mixing bowl, place the Panko breadcrumbs and season with salt and pepper to taste, onion powder, and garlic powder.
Step 2: Mix until everything is combined. Set aside.
Step 3: In a bowl, whisk the egg with the help of a fork.
Step 4: Dip the asparagus pieces in the whisked egg, drain well, and coat with breadcrumbs.
Step 5: Arrange the braided asparagus pieces in an air fryer basket and drizzle some olive oil on top.
Step 6: Cook for about 10 minutes at 180°C.
Step 7: Serve as they are or with crumbled feta cheese and chopped fresh parsley leaves.

PEPPERONI TOASTS

This is a great party food idea, especially if you have a birthday to celebrate with kids and lots of guests.

PREPARATION TIME: 5 MINUTES | **COOKING TIME:** 10 MINUTES
SERVING SIZE: 2 PEOPLE | **PER SERVING:** KCAL: 499; FAT: 32.2G; CARBS: 26.7G; PROTEIN: 25.7G; SUGARS: 3.2G; FIBRE: 4.9G

Ingredients:
- 4 slices of toast bread
- 2 teaspoons butter
- 8 slices of pepperoni
- 100g grated cheese
- 1 teaspoon dried oregano

Instructions:
Step 1: Spread each piece of toast bread with butter and arrange 2 pepperoni slices on each piece of toast bread
Step 2: With the help of your kitchen grater, grate the cheese and place it on top of the pepperoni slices.
Step 3: Sprinkle with some dried oregano and place two pieces at a time in an air fryer basket.
Step 4: Cook for about 10 minutes at 160°C. Serve and enjoy.

ASPARAGUS WITH BACON

You will adore these bacon-wrapped asparagus sticks! They are crispy and golden brown in color, and you will love the crunchy taste and amazing flavour.

PREPARATION TIME: 5 MINUTES | **COOKING TIME: 10 MINUTES**

SERVING SIZE: 2 PEOPLE | **PER SERVING: KCAL: 801; FAT: 59.7G; CARBS: 7.9G; PROTEIN: 56.1G; SUGARS: 2.8G; FIBRE: 3.2G**

Ingredients:

- 300g fresh asparagus
- 15 slices of bacon

Instructions:

Step 1: Take one slice of bacon and carefully wrap around each asparagus.

Step 2: Arrange the bacon-wrapped asparagus pieces in an air fryer basket and air fry for about 10 minutes at 180°C degrees.

Step 3: Cook without any extra oil, the bacon will release enough fat and will develop crispy and crunchy taste. Serve and enjoy.

ASPARAGUS WITH LEMON

Healthy, refreshing, and delicious, you will adore this next flavour combination. Asparagus is great with lemon zest, and you will love every bite of it.

PREPARATION TIME: 5 MINUTES | **COOKING TIME: 10 MINUTES**

SERVING SIZE: 2 PEOPLE | **PER SERVING: KCAL: 91; FAT: 7.2G; CARBS: 6.1G; PROTEIN: 3.4G; SUGARS: 2.8G; FIBRE: 3.2G**

Ingredients:

- 300g fresh asparagus
- Salt and pepper to taste
- 1 tablespoon olive oil
- Zest of 1 lemon
- Juice of 1 lemon
- 1 teaspoon dried dill

Instructions:

Step 1: In a large mixing bowl, place the fresh asparagus that has been washed and drained well.

Step 2: Season with salt and pepper to taste, olive oil, lemon zest, juice, and dried dill.

Step 3: Toss everything together and transfer asparagus pieces into an air fryer basket.

Step 4: Cook for about 10 minutes at 170°C degrees.

Step 5: Serve with sour cream or yoghurt dressing if preferred.

CRAB CAKES

What I love about these crab cakes is that you can make them with canned crab meat and serve them as an appetizer before the main dish. Everyone will enjoy these yummy and delicious savory cakes.

PREPARATION TIME: **5 MINUTES** | COOKING TIME: **15 MINUTES**

SERVING SIZE: **2 PEOPLE** | PER SERVING: **KCAL: 360; FAT: 7.8G; CARBS: 31.1G; PROTEIN: 32.8G; SUGARS: 1.8G; FIBRE: 1.5G**

Ingredients:
- 400g crab meat, drained well
- Salt and pepper to taste
- 1 teaspoon lemon juice
- 1 large egg, room temperature
- 50g breadcrumbs
- 3 tablespoons all-purpose flour
- 1 teaspoon dried dill
- Cooking spray

Instructions:
Step 1: First, in a large mixing bowl add in the well-drained crab meat and season with salt and pepper to taste.

Step 2: Stir in the lemon juice, crack in the egg, and add in the breadcrumbs, flour, and dried dill.

Step 3: Mix until everything is combined and form small crab cakes from the mixture.

Step 4: Spray the air fryer basket a little bit with cooking spray and arrange 4 crab cakes at a time.

Step 5: Spray again with cooking spray to prevent them from sticking and to get an even browning.

Step 6: Cook for about 15 minutes at 180ºC. Be sure to flip the crab cakes halfway through cooking so they will cook evenly.

GARLIC BREAD

This is probably one of everyone's favourite snacks when you want to eat something amazing and delicious but don't want to spend hours in the kitchen to make something yummy for snacking.

PREPARATION TIME: **5 MINUTES** | COOKING TIME: **10 MINUTES**

SERVING SIZE: **2 PEOPLE** | PER SERVING: **KCAL: 154; FAT: 12.2G; CARBS: 10G; PROTEIN: 1.7G; SUGARS: 0.9G; FIBRE: 0.7G**

Ingredients:
- 4 slices of bread
- 2 tablespoons butter
- 1 garlic clove, minced
- 1 tablespoon fresh parsley, chopped finely
- ½ teaspoon dried oregano

Instructions:
Step 1: First, in a small bowl, microwave the butter so that it will become melted. You can do this in a small saucepan over medium heat on the stovetop.

Step 2: In the melted butter, stir in the minced garlic cloves, chopped parsley, and dried oregano.

Step 3: Cut the bread slices into sticks.

Step 4: Using a pastry brush, brush them with the butter and garlic mixture and arrange the breadsticks in an air fryer basket.

Step 5: Cook at 180ºC for about 10 minutes until the breadsticks get golden brown color. Serve and enjoy.

BACON CHIPS

Only one ingredient, but the preparation of it in an air fryer is what makes these bacon chips so delicious and juicy in taste.

PREPARATION TIME: 5 MINUTES | **COOKING TIME: 10 MINUTES**

SERVING SIZE: 2 PEOPLE | **PER SERVING: KCAL: 514; FAT: 39.7G; CARBS: 1.4G; PROTEIN: 35.2G; SUGARS: 0G; FIBRE: 0G**

Ingredients:

- 10 bacon slices, thin

Instructions:

Step 1: Arrange the bacon strips in an air fryer basket.
Step 2: Be careful so the bacon strips don't touch each other. Cook for about 10 minutes at 160ºC until crispy and golden brown.
Step 3: Repeat the same thing until you have used all the bacon.

TAQUITOS

I love how the simplest of ingredients can create the best flavour. These stuffed taquitos are absolutely delicious and quick to put together.

PREPARATION TIME: 5 MINUTES | **COOKING TIME: 10 MINUTES**

SERVING SIZE: 2 PEOPLE | **PER SERVING: KCAL: 579; FAT: 43.6G; CARBS: 25.5G; PROTEIN: 23.3G; SUGARS: 1.5G; FIBRE: 3G**

Ingredients:

- 4 flour tortillas
- 1 tablespoon olive oil
- 150g grated cheese
- 50g marinated mushrooms
- 4 tablespoons cream cheese
- 4 teaspoons mayo

Instructions:

Step 1: First, brush each tortilla with some cream cheese and mayo.
Step 2: Sprinkle with grated cheese and diced marinated mushrooms.
Step 3: Roll each tortilla tightly into a roll and secure it with a toothpick if necessary.
Step 4: Arrange the taquitos in an air fryer basket and drizzle some olive oil.
Step 5: Cook for about 10 minutes at 180ºC. Serve and enjoy.

Please scan the QR code below to access your bonus PDF with all 150 recipes with full coloured photos & beautiful designs alongside!

This is the only way we can get the recipes with coloured photos to you & keep the book as reasonably priced as possible.

Also, once downloaded you can take the PDF with you digitally wherever you go- meaning you can cook these recipes wherever you may be! (As long as you have an air fryer!)

We hope you enjoy and do let us know your feedback!

STEP BY STEP GUIDE TO ACCESS

1. Open Your Phones (Or Any Device You Want The Book On) Back Camera. The Back Camera Is The One You use as if you are taking a picture of someone.
2. Simply point your Camera at the QR code and 'tap' the QR code with your finger to focus the camera.
3. A link / pop up will appear. Simply tap that (and make sure you have internet connection) and the FREE PDF containing all of the coloured images should appear.
4. Now you have access to these FOREVER. Simply 'Bookmark' The tab it opened on, or download the document and take wherever you want.
5. Repeat this on any device you want it on! (If you want it on a laptop, simply email the document to yourself!)

POTATO *Recipes*

— 30 RECIPES —

POTATO FRIES

If you have kids in your home, these potato fries are a healthy snack you can serve and eat without feeling any guilt about it.

PREPARATION TIME: 10 MINUTES | **COOKING TIME: 20 MINUTES**
SERVING SIZE: 2 PEOPLE | **PER SERVING: KCAL: 552; FAT: 5.5G; CARBS: 116.5G; PROTEIN: 12.5G; SUGARS: 8.5G; FIBRE: 18G**

Ingredients:
- 4 large potatoes, washed
- Salt and pepper to taste
- 1 teaspoon dried oregano
- 2 teaspoons olive oil

Instructions:
Step 1: First, wash and peel the potatoes with a potato peeler.
Step 2: Dice the potatoes into 0.5 cm thick slices and then into fries (long strips).
Step 3: Place them in a bowl and season with salt and pepper to taste, dried oregano, and olive oil.
Step 4: Transfer the potato fries to the air fryer basket and cook at 180°C for about 18-20 minutes.
Step 5: Make sure that you shake the air fryer basket halfway through to prevent the fries from sticking and to ensure they cook evenly.

SPICY POTATOES

Spice up your potatoes by adding hot chilli powder. Not only will they look appealing, but they will be crispy and delicious.

PREPARATION TIME: 10 MINUTES | **COOKING TIME: 20 MINUTES**
SERVING SIZE: 2 PEOPLE | **PER SERVING: KCAL: 560; FAT: 5.7G; CARBS: 118.2G; PROTEIN: 12.8G; SUGARS: 9.2G; FIBRE: 18.3G**

Ingredients:
- 4 large potatoes, washed
- Salt and pepper to taste
- 1 teaspoon hot chilli powder
- 1 teaspoon onion powder
- ½ teaspoon garlic powder
- 2 teaspoons olive oil

Instructions:
Step 1: First, wash and peel the potatoes with a potato peeler.
Step 2: Dice the potatoes into medium-thick wedges and place them in a large mixing bowl.
Step 3: Season with salt and pepper to taste, chilli powder, garlic powder, onion powder, and olive oil.
Step 4: Mix until everything is combined.
Step 5: Transfer the potato wedges into the air fryer basket and cook for about 20 minutes at 180°C. Make sure to shake the air fryer basket halfway through to prevent the potatoes from sticking. Serve and enjoy.

CRISPY POTATOES

This potatoes are diced into wedges that are crispy on the outside, tender and delicious on the inside. Seasoned perfectly, you will love every bite of this yummy snack.

PREPARATION TIME: 10 MINUTES | **COOKING TIME: 20 MINUTES**

SERVING SIZE: 2 PEOPLE | **PER SERVING: KCAL: 554; FAT: 5.4G; CARBS: 116.9 G; PROTEIN: 12.5G; SUGARS: 8.9G; FIBRE: 17.9G**

Ingredients:

- 4 large potatoes, washed
- Salt and pepper to taste
- 1 teaspoon dried dill
- 1 teaspoon onion powder
- 2 teaspoons olive oil

Instructions:

Step 1: First, wash and peel the potatoes with a potato peeler.
Step 2: Dice the potatoes into medium-thick wedges and place them in a large mixing bowl.
Step 3: Season with salt and pepper to taste, dried dill, onion powder, and olive oil.
Step 4: Mix until everything is combined.
Step 5: Transfer the potato wedges into the air fryer basket and cook for about 20 minutes at 180°C degrees. Make sure to shake the air fryer basket halfway through to prevent the potatoes from sticking. Serve and enjoy.

CLASSIC AIR FRYER POTATOES

This classic of air-fried potatoes are one of the most made in my home. Just the simplest of ingredients create this delicious and fantastic taste.

PREPARATION TIME: 10 MINUTES | **COOKING TIME: 20 MINUTES**

SERVING SIZE: 2 PEOPLE | **PER SERVING: KCAL: 549; FAT: 5.4G; CARBS: 116G; PROTEIN: 12.4G; SUGARS: 8.5G; FIBRE: 17.7G**

Ingredients:

- 4 large potatoes, washed
- Salt and pepper to taste
- 2 teaspoons olive oil

Instructions:

Step 1: First, wash and peel the potatoes with a potato peeler.
Step 2: Dice the potatoes into cubes 2 cm big in size.
Step 3: Place the potato pieces in a large mixing bowl and season with salt and pepper to taste.
Step 4: Drizzle with olive oil and toss everything until combined.
Step 5: Transfer the potato pieces in the air fryer basket and cook for about 20 minutes at 180°C degrees.
Step 6: After 10 minutes of cooking, remove the air fryer basket and shake the potatoes to prevent them from sticking and to bring even cooking on each side. Serve and enjoy.

JUICY AIR FRYER POTATOES

Side dishes or a potato snack don't mean it has to be complicated. You can prepare a batch of these and share them with the whole family.

PREPARATION TIME: 10 MINUTES | **COOKING TIME: 20 MINUTES**

SERVING SIZE: 2 PEOPLE | **PER SERVING: KCAL: 343; FAT: 5.2G; CARBS: 69G; PROTEIN: 7.6G; SUGARS: 5.5G; FIBRE: 10.6G**

Ingredients:

- 4 medium potatoes, washed
- Salt and pepper to taste
- 1 teaspoon dried onion powder
- ½ teaspoon garlic powder
- 1 teaspoon dried dill
- 2 teaspoons olive oil
- 2 tablespoons fresh parsley, chopped into fine pieces

Instructions:

Step 1: First, wash the potatoes and rinse them well.

Step 2: Dice the potatoes into 2 cm pieces and place them in a large mixing bowl.

Step 3: Season with salt and pepper to taste, dried dill, garlic powder, onion powder, and olive oil.

Step 4: Mix until everything is combined and transfer the diced potatoes into the air fryer basket and cook for about 20 minutes at 180°C.

Step 5: Make sure to shake the air fryer basket halfway through to prevent the potatoes from sticking. Serve with freshly chopped parsley and enjoy.

POTATO CHIPS

Did you know that you can make potato chips in an air fryer? This is a delicious and quick recipe that will become one of your favourite ones.

PREPARATION TIME: 10 MINUTES | **COOKING TIME: 10 MINUTES**

SERVING SIZE: 2 PEOPLE | **PER SERVING: KCAL: 334; FAT: 5.1G; CARBS: 67G; PROTEIN: 7.2G; SUGARS: 4.9G; FIBRE: 10.2G**

Ingredients:

- 4 medium potatoes, washed
- Salt and pepper to taste
- 2-3 teaspoons olive oil

Instructions:

Step 1: First, wash the potatoes and rinse them well. Peel them with potato peeler and slice them thinly on a mandoline.

Step 2: Place them in a large mixing bowl. with

Step 3: Season salt and pepper to taste and olive oil.

Step 4: Transfer the potato slices into the air fryer basket and cook for about 10 minutes at 180°C.

Step 5: Make sure to shake the air fryer basket halfway through to prevent the potatoes from sticking. Serve and enjoy.

BEST AIR FRYER POTATOES

For this recipe, I am using baby potatoes, and I am just cutting them in half. I love the crispy exterior and tender and juicy interior of these potatoes, and I am sure you and your guests will adore them too.

PREPARATION TIME: 10 MINUTES | **COOKING TIME: 20 MINUTES**

SERVING SIZE: 2 PEOPLE | **PER SERVING: KCAL: 192, FAT: 4.9G; CARBS: 32.6G; PROTEIN: 6.7G; SUGARS: 0.6G; FIBRE: 6.4G**

Ingredients:

- 500g baby potatoes,
- Salt and pepper to taste
- 1 teaspoon paprika powder
- 1 teaspoon onion powder
- ½ teaspoon garlic powder
- 2 teaspoons olive oil

Instructions:

Step 1: First, wash the baby potatoes and rinse them well.
Step 2: Dice the baby potatoes in half and place them in a large mixing bowl.
Step 3: Season with salt and pepper to taste, paprika powder, garlic powder, onion powder, and olive oil.
Step 4: Mix until everything is combined and transfer the diced potatoes into the air fryer basket and cook for about 20 minutes at 180°C degrees.
Step 5: Make sure to shake the air fryer basket halfway through to prevent the potatoes from sticking. Serve and enjoy.

POTATOES AND CHEESE

You will love these potato slices with cheese because they are very delicious, crispy and cheesy.

PREPARATION TIME: 10 MINUTES | **COOKING TIME: 20 MINUTES**

SERVING SIZE: 2 PEOPLE | **PER SERVING: KCAL: 394; FAT: 19.2G; CARBS: 40G; PROTEIN: 16.7G; SUGARS: 3.1G; FIBRE: 6G**

Ingredients:

- 500g potatoes
- Salt and pepper to taste
- 1 teaspoon olive oil
- 100g grated cheddar cheese

Instructions:

Step 1: First, wash the potatoes and pat dry them well.
Step 2: Cut them with sharp knife into 2-3 cm pieces.
Step 3: Place the potatoes in the air fryer basket and season with salt and pepper to taste. Drizzle with some oil or spray with cooking spray
Step 5: Cook at 170°C for about 20 minutes.
Step 6: Right before serving, sprinkle grated cheese while the potatoes are still warm. Serve and enjoy.

POTATO CRUNCHIES

*Why crunchies? Because they are very crunchy, delicious, and easy to make.
You will adore this next potato recipe as much as my kids do.*

PREPARATION TIME: 10 MINUTES | **COOKING TIME: 10 MINUTES**

SERVING SIZE: 2 PEOPLE | **PER SERVING: KCAL: 368; FAT: 6.7G; CARBS: 70.8G; PROTEIN: 8.7G; SUGARS: 7G; FIBRE: 11.1G**

Ingredients:
- 4 medium potatoes, washed
- Salt and pepper to taste
- 2 teaspoons olive oil
- 1 tablespoon ketchup
- 1 tablespoon mustard

Instructions:
Step 1: First, wash the potatoes and rinse them well. Peel them with potato peeler and dice them into 2 cm pieces.
Step 2: Transfer them into a large mixing bowl.
Step 3: Season with salt and pepper to taste, ketchup, mustard, and olive oil.
Step 4: Transfer the potato pieces to the air fryer basket and cook for about 20 minutes at 180°C.
Step 5: Make sure to shake the air fryer basket halfway through to prevent the potatoes from sticking. Serve and enjoy.

BBQ SAUCE POTATOES

*If you love some good air-fried potatoes, you have to try these barbeque-inspired flavours.
They are crispy and tender at the same time, making them the perfect party food.*

PREPARATION TIME: 10 MINUTES | **COOKING TIME: 10 MINUTES**

SERVING SIZE: 2 PEOPLE | **PER SERVING: KCAL: 358; FAT: 5.2G; CARBS: 72.6G; PROTEIN: 7.2G; SUGARS: 9G; FIBRE: 10.3G**

Ingredients:
- 4 medium potatoes, washed
- Salt and pepper to taste
- 2 teaspoons olive oil
- 2 tablespoons BBQ sauce

Instructions:
Step 1: First, wash the potatoes and rinse them well. Peel them with potato peeler and dice them into 2 cm pieces.
Step 2: Transfer them into a large mixing bowl.
Step 3: Season with salt and pepper to taste, BBQ sauce, and olive oil.
Step 4: Transfer the potato pieces to the air fryer basket and cook for about 20 minutes at 180°C.
Step 5: Make sure to shake the air fryer basket halfway through to prevent the potatoes from sticking. Serve and enjoy.

HOT SAUCE POTATOES

I love to serve these air fryer hot sauce potatoes to all my friends who love spicy food.

- **PREPARATION TIME: 10 MINUTES**
- **COOKING TIME: 10 MINUTES**
- **SERVING SIZE: 2 PEOPLE** | **PER SERVING: KCAL: 351; FAT: 5.7G; CARBS: 69.3G; PROTEIN: 7.8G; SUGARS: 5.2G; FIBRE: 10.7G**

Ingredients:

- 4 medium potatoes, washed
- Salt and pepper to taste
- 2 teaspoons olive oil
- 2 tablespoons hot chilli sauce

Instructions:

Step 1: First, wash the potatoes and rinse them well. Peel them with potato peeler and dice them into 2 cm pieces.
Step 2: Transfer them into a large mixing bowl.
Step 3: Season with salt and pepper to taste, hot chilli sauce, and olive oil.
Step 4: Transfer the potato pieces to the air fryer basket and cook for about 20 minutes at 180°C.
Step 5: Make sure to shake the air fryer basket halfway through to prevent the potatoes from sticking. Serve and enjoy.

CRISPY SWEET POTATOES

Sweet potatoes are also great in an air fryer. They turn out perfectly crispy and delicious for every snack craving.

- **PREPARATION TIME: 10 MINUTES**
- **COOKING TIME: 20 MINUTES**
- **SERVING SIZE: 2 PEOPLE** | **PER SERVING: KCAL: 222 FAT: 4.9G; CARBS: 42.9G; PROTEIN: 2.6G; SUGARS: 1.1G; FIBRE: 6.3G**

Ingredients:

- 2 sweet potatoes, washed
- Salt and pepper to taste
- 2 teaspoons olive oil
- 1 teaspoon garlic powder

Instructions:

Step 1: First, wash the sweet potatoes and rinse them well. Peel them with potato peeler and dice them into 2 cm pieces.
Step 2: Transfer potatoes into a large mixing bowl.
Step 3: Season with salt and pepper to taste, garlic powder, and olive oil.
Step 4: Transfer the potato pieces to the air fryer basket and cook for about 20 minutes at 180°C.
Step 5: Make sure to shake the air fryer basket halfway through to prevent the potatoes from sticking. Serve and enjoy.

MASHED SWEET POTATOES

Once you will try these mashed sweet potatoes you will forget about the classic ones. Boiling potatoes are reducing the "potato flavour." Try out this recipe to enjoy the maximum of the sweet potato flavour.

PREPARATION TIME: **10 MINUTES** | COOKING TIME: **20 MINUTES**

SERVING SIZE: **2 PEOPLE** | PER SERVING: **KCAL: 226; FAT: 4.9G; CARBS: 43G; PROTEIN: 3.2G; SUGARS: 2.1G; FIBRE: 6.2G**

Ingredients:

- 2 sweet potatoes, washed
- Salt and pepper to taste
- 2 teaspoons butter
- 50 ml whole milk

Instructions:

Step 1: First, wash the sweet potatoes and poke each several times with fork.
Step 2: Transfer them into an air fryer basket.
Step 3: Cook for about 20-25 minutes at 200°C degrees.
Step 4: Remove the potatoes from air fryer and let them cool slightly.
Step 5: Peel them completely and mash them in a bowl with the help of a potato masher or fork.
Step 6: Stir in the salt and pepper to taste, butter, and whole milk until creamy and delicious. Serve and enjoy.

SWEET POTATO CHIPS

Once you try these delicious sweet potato chips, you will forget about the regular potato chips. Decadent and rich.

PREPARATION TIME: **10 MINUTES** | COOKING TIME: **20 MINUTES**

SERVING SIZE: **2 PEOPLE** | PER SERVING: **KCAL: 217; FAT: 4.9G; CARBS: 41.9G; PROTEIN: 2.3G; SUGARS: 0.8G; FIBRE: 6.2G**

Ingredients:

- 2 sweet potatoes, washed
- Salt and pepper to taste
- 2 teaspoons olive oil

Instructions:

Step 1: First, wash the sweet potatoes and rinse them well. Peel them with potato peeler and slice thin slices with a mandoline slicer.
Step 2: Transfer them into a large mixing bowl.
Step 3: Season with salt and pepper to taste, and olive oil.
Step 4: Transfer the potato pieces to the air fryer basket and cook for about 20 minutes at 180°C.
Step 5: Make sure to shake the air fryer basket halfway through to prevent the potatoes from sticking. Serve and enjoy.

HASSELBACK SWEET POTATOES

These stuffed Hasselback sweet potatoes are everything you want to serve on your next festive table. They are easy and delicious side dish that will feed a crowd.

PREPARATION TIME: 10 MINUTES | **COOKING TIME: 20 MINUTES**

SERVING SIZE: 2 PEOPLE | **PER SERVING: KCAL: 548; FAT: 31.1G; CARBS: 43G; PROTEIN: 24.1G; SUGARS: 1G; FIBRE: 6.2G**

Ingredients:

- 2 sweet potatoes, washed
- Salt and pepper to taste
- 2 teaspoons butter
- 50g bacon, diced
- 100g grated cheese
- 1 tablespoon fresh parsley, chopped finely

Instructions:

Step 1: First, wash the sweet potatoes and poke each several times with fork.
Step 2: Transfer them into an air fryer basket.
Step 3: Cook for about 20-25 minutes at 200°C.
Step 4: Remove the potatoes from air fryer and let them cool slightly.
Step 5: Cut them in the centre, but not all the way through, squishing the sides to middle open them.
Step 6: Stuff them with diced bacon and sprinkle some grated cheese on top.
Step 7: Cook them again in the air fryer for 5 minutes at 180°C degrees. Serve them with freshly chopped parsley and enjoy.

SMASHED POTATOES

This next recipe is great for entertaining. The potatoes are cooked then smashed with the help of a glass. Brush with butter for even crispier texture.

PREPARATION TIME: 10 MINUTES | **COOKING TIME: 20 MINUTES**

SERVING SIZE: 2 PEOPLE | **PER SERVING: KCAL: 298; FAT: 17.5G; CARBS: 31.1G; PROTEIN: 6.6G; SUGARS: 0G; FIBRE: 6.3G**

Ingredients:

- 500g baby potatoes
- Salt and pepper to taste
- 3 tablespoons butter

Instructions:

Step 1: First, wash the potatoes and pat dry them well.
Step 2: Transfer them into an air fryer basket. Season with salt and pepper to taste.
Step 3: Cook for about 15 minutes at 180°C.
Step 4: Remove the baby potatoes from the air fryer and with the help of the bottom of the glass smash them.
Step 5: Brush the smashed potatoes with melted butter and return them back in the air fryer.
Step 6: Let them cook for about 5 more minutes at 180°C and serve to enjoy.

SWEET POTATO FRIES

I love to give my kid healthy and delicious alternatives to the most popular junk foods. You will adore these sweet potato fries.

PREPARATION TIME: 10 MINUTES | **COOKING TIME: 20 MINUTES**
SERVING SIZE: 2 PEOPLE | **PER SERVING: KCAL: 217; FAT: 4.9G; CARBS: 41.9G; PROTEIN: 2.3G; SUGARS: 0.8G; FIBRE: 6.2G**

Ingredients:
- 2 sweet potatoes, washed
- Salt and pepper to taste
- 2 teaspoons olive oil
- 1 teaspoon paprika powder

Instructions:
Step 1: First, wash the sweet potatoes and rinse them well. Peel them with a potato peeler and dice them into sticks to get the fry shape.
Step 2: Transfer them into a large mixing bowl.
Step 3: Season with salt and pepper to taste, paprika powder, and olive oil.
Step 4: Transfer the potato pieces to the air fryer basket and cook for about 20 minutes at 180°C.
Step 5: Make sure to shake the air fryer basket halfway through to prevent the potatoes from sticking. Serve and enjoy.

SWEET POTATO CAKES

You will love these sweet potato cakes because they are delicious and perfect for snacking with your favourite people.

PREPARATION TIME: 10 MINUTES | **COOKING TIME: 20 MINUTES**
SERVING SIZE: 2 PEOPLE | **PER SERVING: KCAL: 395; FAT: 7.8G; CARBS: 72.9G; PROTEIN: 9.3G; SUGARS: 2.5G; FIBRE: 7.9G**

Ingredients:
- 2 sweet potatoes, washed
- Salt and pepper to taste
- 2 teaspoons olive oil
- 1 large egg, room temperature
- 70g all-purpose flour
- 1 teaspoon baking powder
- 1 carrot, grated

Instructions:
Step 1: First, wash the sweet potatoes and peel them with potato peeler.
Step 2: Peel the carrot well and grate it with the help of a kitchen grater. Grate the sweet potatoes too.
Step 3: Place the grated carrot and sweet potatoes in a large mixing bowl. Stir in the olive oil, salt and pepper to taste, egg, flour, baking powder; mix until combined.
Step 4: Lay down a piece of parchment paper in your air fryer and add tablespoonful of the sweet potato mixture to form the sweet potato cakes.
Step 5: Spray with cooking spray and cook at 180°C for about 15 minutes.
Step 6: Flip the sweet potato cakes on the other side and cook for 5 more minutes until crispy and delicious. Serve with Greek yoghurt if desired and enjoy.

SWEET POTATO GARLIC CRISPS

If you love seasoned snacks, you will adore these sweet potato garlic infused crisps. They are delicious and infused with the right amount of garlic.

PREPARATION TIME: **10 MINUTES** | COOKING TIME: **20 MINUTES**

SERVING SIZE: **2 PEOPLE** | PER SERVING: **KCAL: 222; FAT: 4.9G; CARBS: 42.9G; PROTEIN: 2.6G; SUGARS: 1.1G; FIBRE: 6.3G**

Ingredients:

- 2 sweet potatoes, washed
- Salt and pepper to taste
- 2 teaspoons olive oil
- 1 teaspoon garlic powder
- 1 teaspoon chilli flakes

Instructions:

Step 1: First, wash the sweet potatoes and peel them with a potato peeler.
Step 2: Dice them into sticks and place them in a large mixing bowl.
Step 3: Season with salt and pepper to taste, garlic powder and chilli flakes.
Step 4: Drizzle the olive oil and transfer them into an air fryer basket.
Step 5: Cook for about 15 minutes at 170ºC degrees. Serve and enjoy with your favourite sauce.

SWEET POTATO CASSEROLE

Easy, quick and tasty side dish that your guests will love. Make this on a busy working day to have something warm and cosy for your dinner.

PREPARATION TIME: **10 MINUTES** | COOKING TIME: **20 MINUTES**

SERVING SIZE: **2 PEOPLE** | PER SERVING: **KCAL: 735; FAT: 57.2G; CARBS: 46.3G; PROTEIN: 12.9G; SUGARS: 0.9G; FIBRE: 6.2G**

Ingredients:

- 2 sweet potatoes, washed
- Salt and pepper to taste
- 2 teaspoons olive oil
- 250 ml heavy cream
- 50 ml water
- 50g grated parmesan cheese

Instructions:

Step 1: First, wash the sweet potatoes and peel them with potato peeler.
Step 2: Dice them in ½ cm thick slices.
Step 3: Take a round casserole pan that will fit your air fryer and grease with olive oil.
Step 4: Arrange the sweet potato slices around the casserole pan and pour in the water and heavy cream.
Step 5: Finally cook for about 15 minutes at 170ºC and sprinkle with grated parmesan cheese.
Step 6: Continue with cooking for 5 more minutes at 170ºC and serve to enjoy.

"GRILLED" SWEET POTATO SLICES

You will love these grilled-like sweet potato slices. You can brush them with olive oil or use butter just like I do in my recipe. They are always great for entertaining.

PREPARATION TIME: 10 MINUTES | **COOKING TIME: 15 MINUTES**

SERVING SIZE: 2 PEOPLE | **PER SERVING: KCAL: 282; FAT: 11.8G; CARBS: 42.6G; PROTEIN: 2.6G; SUGARS: 0.8G; FIBRE: 6.3G**

Ingredients:
- 2 sweet potatoes, washed
- Salt and pepper to taste
- 2 tablespoons butter, melted
- 1 tablespoon parsley, freshly chopped
- 1 garlic clove, minced
- 1 teaspoon dried mint

Instructions:
Step 1: First, wash the sweet potatoes and peel them with potato peeler.
Step 2: Dice them in 1 cm thick slices.
Step 3: In a large bowl, mix the melted butter, chopped parsley, minced garlic clove, salt and pepper to taste, and dried mint.
Step 4: With the help of a pastry brush, brush each slice of sweet potato and arrange the slices in an air fryer basket.
Step 5: Cook at 180°C for about 15-17 minutes. Serve and enjoy.

HASSELBACK POTATOES

I love some great Hasselback potatoes. They are delicious, easy to put together and will definitely feed a crowd.

PREPARATION TIME: 10 MINUTES | **COOKING TIME: 20 MINUTES**

SERVING SIZE: 2 PEOPLE | **PER SERVING: KCAL: 601; FAT: 27.5G; CARBS: 60.8G; PROTEIN: 28.7G; SUGARS: 5G; FIBRE: 9.6G**

Ingredients:
- 2 large potatoes, washed
- Salt and pepper to taste
- 50g bacon, diced
- 100g grated cheese
- 50g broccoli florets
- 1 tablespoon fresh parsley, chopped finely

Instructions:
Step 1: First, wash the potatoes and poke each several times with fork.
Step 2: Transfer them into an air fryer basket.
Step 3: Cook for about 20-25 minutes at 200 C degrees.
Step 4: Remove the potatoes from air fryer and let them cool slightly.
Step 5: Cut them in the centre, but not all the way through squishing the sides so to middle open them.
Step 6: Stuff them with diced bacon, broccoli florets and sprinkle some grated cheese on top.
Step 7: Cook them again in the air fryer for 5 minutes at 180°C degrees. Serve them with freshly chopped parsley and enjoy.

SMASHED GARLICKY POTATOES

If you love some good garlicky potatoes, you will adore this next flavour combination. Butter, garlic, and some dry herbs – perfect for everyone's taste.

- PREPARATION TIME: **10 MINUTES** | COOKING TIME: **20 MINUTES**
- SERVING SIZE: **2 PEOPLE** | PER SERVING: **KCAL: 305; FAT: 17.6G; CARBS: 32.6G; PROTEIN: 6.9G; SUGARS: 0.1G; FIBRE: 6.7G**

Ingredients:

- 500g baby potatoes
- Salt and pepper to taste
- 2 garlic cloves, minced
- 2 teaspoons dried basil
- 1 teaspoon dried oregano
- 3 tablespoons butter

Instructions:

Step 1: First, wash the potatoes and pat dry them well.
Step 2: Transfer them into an air fryer basket. Season with salt and pepper to taste.
Step 3: Cook for about 15 minutes at 180°C.
Step 4: Remove the baby potatoes from the air fryer and with the help of the bottom of the glass smash them.
Step 5: Brush the smashed potatoes with melted butter mixed with minced garlic cloves, dried basil, and dried oregano, then return them back in the air fryer.
Step 6: Let them cook for about 5 more minutes at 180°C and serve to enjoy.

DOMINO POTATOES

I love these domino potatoes because they are fun to make, and your guests will enjoy the taste and flavour.

- PREPARATION TIME: **10 MINUTES** | COOKING TIME: **15 MINUTES**
- SERVING SIZE: **2 PEOPLE** | PER SERVING: **KCAL: 325; FAT: 17.5G; CARBS: 39.3G; PROTEIN: 4.4G; SUGARS: 2.9G; FIBRE: 6G**

Ingredients:

- 500g potatoes
- Salt and pepper to taste
- 3 tablespoons butter

Instructions:

Step 1: First, wash the potatoes and pat dry them well.
Step 2: Peel them with potato peeler and dice them as thin as possible in slices.
Step 3: Arrange the potato slices in a piece of baking paper that will fit into your air fryer basket.
Step 4: Season with salt and pepper to taste and brush with melted butter.
Step 5: Air fry for about 15 minutes at 170°C until crispy and delicious and serve to enjoy.

SWEET POTATO TATER TOTS

This is the easiest and tastiest recipe for sweet potato tater tots. They are delicious, easy to make, and fun to prepare.

PREPARATION TIME: **10 MINUTES** | COOKING TIME: **20 MINUTES**

SERVING SIZE: **2 PEOPLE** | PER SERVING: **KCAL: 407; FAT: 10.7G; CARBS: 65.4G; PROTEIN: 13.1G; SUGARS: 1G; FIBRE: 7G**

Ingredients:
- 2 sweet potatoes, washed
- Salt and pepper to taste
- 2 teaspoons olive oil
- 1 large egg, room temperature
- 60g all-purpose flour
- 2 tablespoons grated parmesan cheese

Instructions:
Step 1: First, wash the sweet potatoes and peel them with potato peeler.
Step 2: Grate them with the help of your kitchen grater and place them in a bowl.
Step 3: Season with salt and pepper to taste, olive oil, egg, flour, and grated parmesan cheese.
Step 4: Mix until everything is combined and form small tater tots by taking one or two tablespoons of the sweet potato mixture and making it in an oval shape.
Step 5: Arrange the tater tots in an air fryer basket and spray them with a little cooking spray.
Step 6: Cook for about 15 minutes at 180°C degrees.
Step 7: Serve with your favourite sauce and enjoy.

POTATO BALLS

I love these potato crockets. They are made with mashed potatoes and are perfect to serve as an appetizer.

PREPARATION TIME: **10 MINUTES** | COOKING TIME: **30 MINUTES**

SERVING SIZE: **2 PEOPLE** | PER SERVING: **KCAL: 577; FAT: 12.4G; CARBS: 95.6G; PROTEIN: 21.1G; SUGARS: 6.2G; FIBRE: 10.7G**

Ingredients:
- 2 large potatoes, washed
- Salt and pepper to taste
- 1 medium egg, room temperature
- 50g breadcrumbs
- 50g all-purpose flour
- 50g grated cheese

Instructions:
Step 1: First, wash the potatoes and poke each several times with fork.
Step 2: Transfer them into an air fryer basket.
Step 3: Cook for about 20-25 minutes at 200°C degrees.
Step 4: Remove the potatoes from air fryer and let them cool slightly. Peel the potatoes and mash them with potato masher or with the help of a fork.
Step 5: In the mashed potatoes, stir in the egg, salt and pepper to taste, flour, and grated cheese.
Step 6: Mix all the ingredients together until fully combined and form small balls.
Step 7: Coat them in the breadcrumbs and place in the air fryer basket.
Step 8: Cook for about 10 minutes at 170°C and serve to enjoy.

CHEESY RANCH BABY POTATOES

Simple and delicious you will adore this next recipe. It's absolutely gorgeous and perfect for side dish.

PREPARATION TIME: 10 MINUTES | **COOKING TIME: 20 MINUTES**

SERVING SIZE: 2 PEOPLE | **PER SERVING:** : **KCAL: 362; FAT: 16.8G; CARBS: 31.8G; PROTEIN: 18.9G; SUGARS: 0.3G; FIBRE: 6.3G**

Ingredients:

- 500g baby potatoes
- Salt and pepper to taste
- 1 tablespoon ranch seasoning
- 100g grated cheese

Instructions:

Step 1: First, wash the potatoes and pat dry them well.
Step 2: Transfer them into an air fryer basket. Season with salt and pepper to taste and ranch seasoning.
Step 3: Cook for about 20 minutes at 200 C degrees.
Step 4: Make sure to shake the potatoes in the air fryer basket halfway through.
Step 5: Just 5 minutes before the ending sprinkle with some grated cheese on top. Serve and enjoy.

POTATOES AND SAUSAGES

I really like this dish because it's a lunch or dinner replacer. It has the right amount of carbs, proteins, and everything you need for a cosy meal for the whole family.

PREPARATION TIME: 10 MINUTES | **COOKING TIME: 20 MINUTES**

SERVING SIZE: 2 PEOPLE | **PER SERVING: KCAL: 596; FAT: 35.7G; CARBS: 39.3G; PROTEIN: 28.5G; SUGARS: 2.9G; FIBRE: 6G**

Ingredients:

- 500g potatoes
- Salt and pepper to taste
- 250g sausages

Instructions:

Step 1: First, wash the potatoes and pat dry them well.
Step 2: Cut them with sharp knife into 2-3 cm pieces.
Step 3: Dice the sausages into 2-3 cm pieces as well.
Step 4: Place the potatoes and sausages in the air fryer basket and season with salt and pepper to taste. You don't have to add extra oil because the sausages will release some when cooking.
Step 5: Cook at 170°C for about 20 minutes. Serve and enjoy.

HASSELBACK POTATOES THE OTHER WAY

I really do like these Hasselback potatoes. They are yummy and crispy at the same time and the presentation is quite stunning.

PREPARATION TIME: 10 MINUTES | **COOKING TIME: 20 MINUTES**

SERVING SIZE: 2 PEOPLE | **PER SERVING: KCAL: 295; FAT: 5G; CARBS: 58G; PROTEIN: 6.5G SUGARS: 4.2G; FIBRE: 8.9G**

Ingredients:

- 2 large potatoes
- Salt and pepper to taste
- 2 teaspoons olive oil

Instructions:

Step 1: First, wash the potatoes and pat dry them well.
Step 2: Dice the potatoes every 2-3 mm, being careful not to cut them all the way through.
Step 3: Brush them with olive oil and season them with salt and pepper to taste.
Step 4: Cook for about 20-25 minutes at 200ºC.
Step 5: Serve them with freshly chopped parsley and enjoy.

BACON AND POTATOES

I love this next recipe because it has the two ingredients I love the most – bacon and potatoes. You will adore them together and how quick they cook in an air fryer.

PREPARATION TIME: 10 MINUTES | **COOKING TIME: 20 MINUTES**

SERVING SIZE: 2 PEOPLE | **PER SERVING: KCAL: 416; FAT: 21.1G; CARBS: 31.9G; PROTEIN: 25G; SUGARS: 0G; FIBRE: 6.3G**

Ingredients:

- 500g baby potatoes
- Salt and pepper to taste
- 100g bacon, cut into small cubes

Instructions:

Step 1: First, wash the potatoes and pat dry them well.
Step 2: Transfer them into an air fryer basket. Season with salt and pepper to taste.
Step 3: Cook for about 15 minutes at 180ºC degrees.
Step 4: Make sure to shake the potatoes in the air fryer basket halfway through.
Step 5: Remove the baby potatoes from the air fryer and sprinkle with diced bacon.
Step 6: Cook for 5 more minutes at 170ºC and serve to enjoy.

Please scan the QR code below to access your bonus PDF with all 150 recipes with full coloured photos & beautiful designs alongside!

This is the only way we can get the recipes with coloured photos to you & keep the book as reasonably priced as possible.

Also, once downloaded you can take the PDF with you digitally wherever you go- meaning you can cook these recipes wherever you may be! (As long as you have an air fryer!)

We hope you enjoy and do let us know your feedback!

STEP BY STEP GUIDE TO ACCESS

1. Open Your Phones (Or Any Device You Want The Book On) Back Camera. The Back Camera Is The One You use as if you are taking a picture of someone.
2. Simply point your Camera at the QR code and 'tap' the QR code with your finger to focus the camera.
3. A link / pop up will appear. Simply tap that (and make sure you have internet connection) and the FREE PDF containing all of the coloured images should appear.
4. Now you have access to these FOREVER. Simply 'Bookmark' The tab it opened on, or download the document and take wherever you want.
5. Repeat this on any device you want it on! (If you want it on a laptop, simply email the document to yourself!)

LUNCHES AND DINNERS
Recipes

—— 35 RECIPES ——

HOT CHICKEN WINGS

Let's bring the chicken wings to a whole another level. I love this amazing recipe because it has flavour, taste, and amazing presentation.

PREPARATION TIME: 10 MINUTES | **COOKING TIME: 20 MINUTES**

SERVING SIZE: 2 PEOPLE | **PER SERVING: KCAL: 534; FAT: 23.5G; CARBS: 4.6G; PROTEIN: 72.8G; SUGARS: 3.5G; FIBRE: 0.5G**

Ingredients:

- 500g chicken wings
- Salt and pepper to taste
- 2 teaspoons olive oil
- 1 teaspoon chilli flakes
- 2 tablespoons ketchup
- 1 tablespoon sriracha sauce
- 1 teaspoon chilli powder

Instructions:

Step 1: First, place the chicken wings in a large mixing bowl. If your chicken wings are frozen, thaw them completely before using them.

Step 2: Season with salt and pepper to taste, chilli flakes, sriracha sauce, ketchup, chilli powder, and olive oil.

Step 3: Mix everything together and transfer the chicken wings to the air fryer basket.

Step 4: Cook for about 20 minutes at 180°C.

Step 5: Make sure to shake the air fryer basket halfway through to prevent them from sticking and to develop a crispy exterior on all sides. Serve with your favourite sauce.

CHICKEN WINGS

This classic recipe for chicken wings can be an appetizer but also a delicious and quick dinner idea to feed the whole family.

PREPARATION TIME: 10 MINUTES | **COOKING TIME: 20 MINUTES**

SERVING SIZE: 2 PEOPLE | **PER SERVING: KCAL: 517; FAT: 23.3G; CARBS: 0.5G; PROTEIN: 72.4G; SUGARS: 0G; FIBRE: 0.3G**

Ingredients:

- 500g chicken wings
- Salt and pepper to taste
- 2 teaspoons olive oil
- 1 teaspoon dried oregano
- 1 teaspoon paprika powder

Instructions:

Step 1: First, place the chicken wings in a large mixing bowl. If your chicken wings are frozen, thaw them completely before using them.

Step 2: Season with salt and pepper to taste, olive oil, dried oregano, and paprika powder.

Step 3: Mix everything together and transfer the chicken wing in an air fryer basket.

Step 4: Cook for about 20 minutes at 180°C.

Step 5: Make sure to shake the air fryer basket halfway through to prevent them from sticking and to develop a crispy exterior on all sides. Serve with your favourite sauce.

CHICKEN PARMIGIANA

Everyone's favourite chicken recipe is crispy parmigiana. I love this recipe because it's easy to put together and that tomato sauce on top and mozzarella cheese make it even more delicious.

PREPARATION TIME: 10 MINUTES | **COOKING TIME: 20 MINUTES**

SERVING SIZE: 2 PEOPLE | **PER SERVING: KCAL: 673; FAT: 28.2G; CARBS: 29.3G; PROTEIN: 72.8G; SUGARS: 4.1G; FIBRE: 2.4G**

Ingredients:
- 400g chicken fillets
- Salt and pepper to taste
- 1 teaspoon onion powder
- 1 teaspoon dried oregano
- 1 large egg, lightly whisked
- 2 teaspoons olive oil or cooking spray
- 70g breadcrumbs
- 2 tablespoons grated parmesan cheese
- 4 tablespoons tomato sauce
- 50g mozzarella cheese

Instructions:
Step 1: Season the chicken fillets with salt and pepper to taste.
Step 2: Dip each chicken fillet into a lightly whisked egg.
Step 3: In a bowl, mix the breadcrumbs, onion powder, dried oregano, and grated parmesan cheese.
Step 4: Coat the chicken fillets in the breadcrumb mixture.
Step 5: Arrange the chicken fillets in the air fryer basket and drizzle them with olive oil or spray with cooking spray.
Step 6: Cook for about 10 minutes at 180ºC; flip on the other side and add some tomato sauce and mozzarella cheese.
Step 7: Cook for about 8-10 more minutes and serve to enjoy.

ROASTED CHICKEN

Yes! You can make a whole chicken in an air fryer in a blink of an eye. You will love the juicy meat, crispy skin, and how this delicious chicken is made.

PREPARATION TIME: 10 MINUTES | **COOKING TIME: 45 MINUTES**

SERVING SIZE: 4 PEOPLE | **PER SERVING: KCAL: 527; FAT: 24.3G; CARBS: 0.1G; PROTEIN: 72.4G; SUGARS: 0G; FIBRE: 0.1G**

Ingredients:
- 1 kg whole chicken
- Salt and pepper to taste
- 2 tablespoons butter
- Zest of 1 lemon
- 1 tablespoon fresh parsley, chopped
- 1 teaspoon dried mint

Instructions:
Step 1: In a bowl, mix the butter with the lemon zest, freshly chopped parsley, and dried mint.
Step 2: Pat dry the whole chicken and rub the butter mixture all over the meat.
Step 3: Place the whole chicken in an air fryer basket and cook for about 40-45 minutes at 180ºC.
Step 4: Just 10 minutes before the timer ends, flip the chicken to the other side and cook until crispy and delicious.

CHICKEN WITH BROCCOLI

I love to add some fresh ingredients in the recipes to balance the nutrients and calories. This chicken and broccoli dish will absolutely be loved both by adults and kids.

PREPARATION TIME: 10 MINUTES | **COOKING TIME: 18 MINUTES**

SERVING SIZE: 2 PEOPLE | **PER SERVING: KCAL: 348; FAT: 9G; CARBS: 8.4G; PROTEIN: 56.5G; SUGARS: 2.1G; FIBRE: 3.3G**

Ingredients:

- 500g chicken breast, boneless and skinless
- Salt and pepper to taste
- 1 teaspoon dried mint
- 1 teaspoon olive oil
- 250g broccoli florets

Instructions:

Step 1: First, dice the chicken breasts into small 1 cm cubes.
Step 2: Season them with salt and pepper to taste and dried mint.
Step 3: Transfer the chicken pieces to an air fryer basket and add in the broccoli florets.
Step 4: Drizzle with some olive oil and cook at 180°C for about 10 minutes.
Step 5: Shake the air fryer basket to prevent them from sticking and to develop much crispier crust on the chicken. Continue with cooking for 7-8 minutes more.

GARLIC CHICKEN

If you ask me what I love the most when I cook chicken, I will say that garlic with chicken is my winning flavour combination.

PREPARATION TIME: 10 MINUTES | **COOKING TIME: 20 MINUTES**

SERVING SIZE: 2 PEOPLE | **PER SERVING: KCAL: 314; FAT: 8.6G; CARBS: 2G; PROTEIN: 53.4G; SUGARS: 0.8G; FIBRE: 0.2G**

Ingredients:

- 500g chicken breast, boneless and skinless (approx. 2 chicken breasts)
- Salt and pepper to taste
- 1 teaspoon onion powder
- 1 teaspoon garlic powder
- 1 teaspoon olive oil

Instructions:

Step 1: Cut the chicken breasts in half to make four chicken fillets.
Step 2: Season them with salt and pepper to taste, onion, and garlic powder.
Step 3: Transfer the chicken fillets in an air fryer basket.
Step 4: Drizzle with some olive oil and cook at 180°C for about 10 minutes.
Step 5: Halfway through, flip the chicken pieces on the other side and continue with cooking for 10 minutes more. Serve and enjoy with mashed potatoes.

CRISPY CHICKEN

This is my kid's favourite recipe with chicken, and I love to prepare it in an air fryer. It's crispy and easy to make and always a showstopper.

PREPARATION TIME: 10 MINUTES | **COOKING TIME: 20 MINUTES**

SERVING SIZE: 2 PEOPLE | **PER SERVING:** KCAL: 648; FAT: 26.9G; CARBS: 27.9G; PROTEIN: 70.6G; SUGARS: 3.1G; FIBRE: 1.8G

Ingredients:

- 400g chicken fillets
- Salt and pepper to taste
- 1 teaspoon onion powder
- 1 teaspoon garlic powder
- 1 large egg, lightly whisked
- 2 teaspoons olive oil or cooking spray
- 70g breadcrumbs
- 2 tablespoons grated parmesan cheese

Instructions:

Step 1: Season the chicken fillets with salt and pepper to taste.
Step 2: Dip each chicken fillet into a lightly whisked egg.
Step 3: In a bowl, mix the breadcrumbs, onion powder, garlic powder, and grated parmesan cheese.
Step 4: Coat the chicken fillets in the breadcrumb mixture.
Step 5: Arrange the chicken fillets in the air fryer basket and drizzle them with olive oil or spray with cooking spray.
Step 6: Cook for about 10 minutes at 180°C. Flip the crispy chicken on the other side. Continue with cooking for 10 more minutes. Serve and enjoy.

CHICKEN THIGHS

You can place 4-5 chicken thighs in an air fryer basket, depending on the size of the meat. This recipe is straightforward and perfect when you want to make a cheap meal for the whole family.

PREPARATION TIME: 10 MINUTES | **COOKING TIME: 20 MINUTES**

SERVING SIZE: 2 PEOPLE | **PER SERVING:** KCAL: 523; FAT: 23.9G; CARBS: 0.3G; PROTEIN: 72.4G; SUGARS: 0.2G; FIBRE: 0G

Ingredients:

- 500g chicken thighs
- Salt and pepper to taste
- 1 teaspoon paprika powder
- 1 teaspoon chilli flakes
- 2 teaspoons olive oil
- 1 teaspoon Italian seasonings

Instructions:

Step 1: In a bowl, place the chicken thighs and pat dry them with kitchen paper.
Step 2: Season them with salt and pepper to taste paprika powder, chilli powder, and Italian seasonings, and drizzle with olive oil.
Step 3: Transfer the chicken thighs to an air fryer basket and cook for about 20 minutes at 180°C.
Step 4: Make sure to shake the air fryer basket halfway through to have much crispier and juicier chicken. Serve and enjoy.

CHICKEN IN ORANGE SAUCE

If you like to bring chicken to a whole other level, you should give this recipe a try. The orange juice and zest will bring a fresh taste, fantastic flavour, and crispy and juicy crust.

PREPARATION TIME: **10 MINUTES** | COOKING TIME: **20 MINUTES**

SERVING SIZE: **2 PEOPLE** | PER SERVING: **KCAL: 546; FAT: 23.3G; CARBS: 6.5G; PROTEIN: 73.3G; SUGARS: 0G; FIBRE: 0.3G**

Ingredients:
- 500g chicken fillets
- Salt and pepper to taste
- 2 teaspoons olive oil
- Juice and zest of 1 orange
- 1 garlic clove, minced
- 2 tablespoons all-purpose flour

Instructions:
Step 1: Season the chicken pieces with salt and pepper to taste.
Step 2: In a bowl, mix the orange juice and zest with the minced garlic cloves and dip the chicken pieces in the orange mixture. Let them steep for 5 minutes.
Step 3: Drain the chicken pieces from the liquid and coat them with a little bit of flour.
Step 4: Arrange the chicken pieces in an air fryer basket and drizzle some olive oil.
Step 5: Cook for about 10 minutes at 180°C. Flip them on the other side to cook for about 10 more minutes. Serve and enjoy with cooked basmati rice.

CHICKEN RISSOLES

Another chicken recipe that is perfect in an air fryer. Delicious and nutritious. You will adore every bite of these rissoles.

PREPARATION TIME: **10 MINUTES** | COOKING TIME: **20 MINUTES**

SERVING SIZE: **2 PEOPLE** | PER SERVING: **679; FAT: 25.2G; CARBS: 25.3G; PROTEIN: 84.4G; SUGARS: 4.7G; FIBRE: 2.8G**

Ingredients:
- 500g ground chicken
- Salt and pepper to taste
- 25g grated parmesan cheese
- 50g breadcrumbs
- 1 large egg, room temperature
- 1 courgette, washed and grated finely
- 1 small carrot, peeled and grated
- 1 small shallot, diced finely

Instructions:
Step 1: In a large mixing bowl, place the ground chicken and season with salt and pepper to taste.
Step 2: With the kitchen grater, finely grate the courgette and carrot and add them to the ground chicken mixture.
Step 3: Add in the egg, parmesan cheese, breadcrumbs, and diced shallot.
Step 4: Mix everything together until thoroughly combined. Form small patties using your hands.
Step 5: Arrange them in an air fryer basket and cook for about 18-20 minutes at 180°C degrees. Serve and enjoy with your favourite sauce.

CHICKEN MEATBALLS

I love some chicken meatballs. These are classic chicken meatballs that you can make for every party celebration or just whenever you crave some for dinner.

PREPARATION TIME: **10 MINUTES** | COOKING TIME: **20 MINUTES**

SERVING SIZE: **2 PEOPLE** | PER SERVING: **KCAL: 717; FAT: 27.7G; CARBS: 8.5G; PROTEIN: 73.8G; SUGARS: 0.3G; FIBRE: 0.2G**

Ingredients:
- 500g ground chicken
- Salt and pepper to taste
- 1 large egg, room temperature
- ½ teaspoon mustard
- 1 tablespoon ketchup
- 1 teaspoon dried oregano
- 50g breadcrumbs

Instructions:
Step 1: In a large mixing bowl, mix the ground chicken, salt and pepper to taste, egg, mustard, ketchup, dried oregano, and breadcrumbs.

Step 2: With the help of your hand, mix everything together until fully combined.

Step 3: Form small meatballs with the help of your hands and arrange them in an air fryer basket.

Step 4: Optional: spray them with cooking oil if you want.

Step 5: Cook for about 18 minutes at 170°C. Serve and enjoy with a salad or your favourite sauce.

CRISPY CHICKEN TENDERS

These chicken tenders are delicious, easy to make, and most importantly, everyone will love them.

PREPARATION TIME: **10 MINUTES** | COOKING TIME: **20 MINUTES**

SERVING SIZE: **2 PEOPLE** | PER SERVING: **KCAL: 717; FAT: 27.7G; CARBS: 8.5G; PROTEIN: 73.8G; SUGARS: 0.3G; FIBRE: 0.2G**

Ingredients:
- 500g chicken tenders
- Salt and pepper to taste
- 1 teaspoon paprika powder
- 1 large egg, lightly whisked
- 50g Panko breadcrumbs
- 2 teaspoons olive oil
- 1 teaspoon Italian seasonings

Instructions:
Step 1: In a bowl, mix the Panko breadcrumbs with the paprika powder and Italian seasonings.

Step 2: Season the chicken tenders with salt and pepper to taste.

Step 3: Lightly whisk the egg with the help of a fork and dip each piece of chicken tender into the whisked egg.

Step 4: Coat the chicken tenders with the breadcrumb mixture and arrange each piece in an air fryer basket.

Step 5: Drizzle the olive oil on top and cook at 180°C for about 18-20 minutes. Serve and enjoy

CHICKEN DRUMSTICKS

If you love chicken drumsticks, you will absolutely adore the following recipe. It's crispy, juicy, and delicious.

PREPARATION TIME: 10 MINUTES | **COOKING TIME: 20 MINUTES**

SERVING SIZE: 2 PEOPLE | **PER SERVING: KCAL: 449; FAT: 14.8G; CARBS: 5.4G; PROTEIN: 69.6G; SUGARS: 4G; FIBRE: 0.4G**

Ingredients:

- 500g chicken drumsticks
- Salt and pepper to taste
- 1 teaspoon mustard
- 2 tablespoons ketchup
- 1 teaspoon onion powder

Instructions:

Step 1: In a bowl, place the chicken drumsticks and pat dry them with kitchen paper.
Step 2: Season them with salt and pepper to taste and coat them with mustard, onion powder, and ketchup.
Step 3: Transfer them to an air fryer basket and cook for about 20 minutes at 180°C.
Step 4: Halfway through cooking, shake the air fryer basket to prevent them from sticking. Serve and enjoy.

TURKEY MEATBALLS

These turkey meatballs are everything you need for Thanksgiving or any time of the year. They are quick, easy, and super delicious with a special surprise inside.

PREPARATION TIME: 10 MINUTES | **COOKING TIME: 20 MINUTES**

SERVING SIZE: 2 PEOPLE | **PER SERVING: KCAL: 763; FAT: 42G; CARBS: 22.2G; PROTEIN: 82.3G; SUGARS: 4.4G; FIBRE: 1.6G**

Ingredients:

- 500g ground turkey
- Salt and pepper to taste
- 1 large egg, room temperature
- 100g feta cheese, crumbled
- 1 teaspoon onion powder
- ½ teaspoon garlic powder
- 1 teaspoon dried oregano
- 50g breadcrumbs

Instructions:

Step 1: In a large mixing bowl, mix the ground turkey, salt and pepper to taste, egg, onion powder, garlic powder, dried oregano, and breadcrumbs. Crumble the feta cheese on top.
Step 2: With the help of your hand, mix everything together until fully combined.
Step 3: Form small meatballs with the help of your hands and arrange them in an air fryer basket.
Step 4: Optional: spray them with cooking oil if you want.
Step 5: Cook for about 18 minutes at 170°C. Serve and enjoy with a salad or your favourite sauce.

CHICKEN SCHNITZEL

Whenever you crave some chicken schnitzel for lunch, this recipe is foolproof and the one you want to make over and over again.

PREPARATION TIME: 10 MINUTES | **COOKING TIME: 20 MINUTES**

SERVING SIZE: 2 PEOPLE | **PER SERVING: KCAL: 681; FAT: 34G; CARBS: 46.6G; PROTEIN: 30.5G; SUGARS: 3.8G; FIBRE: 8.3G**

Ingredients:
- 2 chicken schnitzels
- Salt and pepper to taste
- 40g all-purpose flour
- 1 large egg, lightly whisked
- 50g Panko breadcrumbs
- 2 tablespoons grated parmesan cheese
- 2 teaspoons olive oil

Instructions:
Step 1: Season the chicken schnitzels with salt and pepper to taste.
Step 2: Coat them well in all-purpose flour and cover each side with flour.
Step 3: In a bowl, crack in the egg and lightly whisk it with the help of a fork.
Step 4: Dip the chicken schnitzels in the whisked egg.
Step 5: In another bowl, mix the Panko breadcrumbs with the grated parmesan cheese and coat the chicken fillets well.
Step 6: Transfer them to an air fryer basket and drizzle some olive oil on top. Cook for about 20 minutes at 180°C.

CHICKEN NUGGETS

Did you know that you can make chicken nuggets in an air fryer? These are much healthier than those in fast food restaurants.

PREPARATION TIME: 10 MINUTES | **COOKING TIME: 20 MINUTES**

SERVING SIZE: 2 PEOPLE | **PER SERVING: KCAL: 372; FAT: 11.6G; CARBS: 5.6G; PROTEIN: 43.4G; SUGARS: 0.7G; FIBRE: 0.3G**

Ingredients:
- 400g chicken breast
- Salt and pepper to taste
- 1 teaspoon onion powder
- 1 teaspoon paprika powder
- ½ teaspoon garlic powder
- ½ teaspoon dried dill
- 70g panko breadcrumbs
- 2 teaspoons olive oil

Instructions:
Step 1: Dice the chicken breasts into 2-3 cm pieces and season them with salt and pepper to taste.
Step 2: In a large mixing bowl, mix the breadcrumbs with the onion powder, paprika powder, garlic powder, and dried dill, then dip each piece of chicken to coat well.
Step 3: Arrange the chicken nuggets in an air fryer basket and drizzle some olive oil on top.
Step 4: Cook for about 15-17 minutes at 180°C. Enjoy with your favourite dipping sauce or cooked basmati rice.

CHICKEN AND PROSCIUTTO

I love to serve these chicken and prosciutto bites whenever I have special guests around. They are quick, delicious, and have excellent presentation.

- PREPARATION TIME: **10 MINUTES** | COOKING TIME: **20 MINUTES**
- SERVING SIZE: **2 PEOPLE** | PER SERVING: **KCAL: 319; FAT: 11.6G; CARBS: 0.6G; PROTEIN: 49.7G; SUGARS: 0G; FIBRE: 0G**

Ingredients:

- 400g chicken breast
- Salt and pepper to taste
- Zest of 1 lime
- 2 teaspoons olive oil
- 70g prosciutto

Instructions:

Step 1: Dice the chicken breast into 2-3 cm pieces and season them with salt and pepper to taste.

Step 2: Season with lime zest, then wrap each piece carefully into a prosciutto slice.

Step 3: Seal the edges with the help of a toothpick and arrange all pieces in an air fryer basket.

Step 4: Drizzle some olive oil on top and cook the chicken pieces at 180°C for about 18 minutes. Serve and enjoy with some honey mustard sauce, ranch dressing, or your favourite go-to side dish.

CHICKEN TANDOORI

You can make this chicken tandoori with any kind of chicken meat. I love to make it with chicken drumsticks so everyone can enjoy this yummy dinner.

- PREPARATION TIME: **10 MINUTES** | COOKING TIME: **20 MINUTES**
- SERVING SIZE: **2 PEOPLE** | PER SERVING: **KCAL: 296; FAT: 12.8G; CARBS: 11.3G; PROTEIN: 33G; SUGARS: 2.4G; FIBRE: 0G**

Ingredients:

- 4 chicken drumsticks
- Salt and pepper to taste
- 120g Greek yoghurt
- 70 tandoori paste
- 1 teaspoon olive oil

Instructions:

Step 1: Season the chicken drumsticks with salt and pepper to taste.

Step 2: In a large shallow bowl, mix the Greek yoghurt and tandoori paste, then coat each chicken drumstick into the mixture.

Step 3: Drain them well from the coating mixture and arrange the pieces in an air fryer basket.

Step 4: Cook at 180°C for about 10 minutes. Flip on the other side and cook for 10 more minutes, until crispy and delicious. Serve and enjoy with your favourite salad.

CHICKEN AND VEGGIES

If you have kids at home, you probably want to serve healthy meals to your little ones. This recipe is nutritious and perfect for healthy lunch or dinner.

PREPARATION TIME: 10 MINUTES | **COOKING TIME: 20 MINUTES**

SERVING SIZE: 2 PEOPLE | **PER SERVING: KCAL: 538; FAT: 20.1G; CARBS: 24.3G; PROTEIN: 64G; SUGARS: 9.5G; FIBRE: 7.5G**

Ingredients:

- 400g chicken breasts
- Salt and pepper to taste
- 1 onion, diced
- 150g broccoli florets
- 2 carrots, peeled and diced
- 100g peas
- 1 garlic clove, minced
- 1 teaspoon dried oregano
- 2 teaspoons olive oil

Instructions:

Step 1: Cut the chicken meat into bite size pieces.
Step 2: Place the chicken pieces in a large mixing bowl. Add in the diced onion, broccoli florets, diced carrots, peas, minced garlic clove, dried oregano, salt and pepper to taste, and olive oil.
Step 3: Toss everything together until mixed. Transfer to an air fryer basket.
Step 4: Cook for about 17-20 minutes at 180ºC.
Step 5: Make sure to shake the air fryer basket halfway through cooking to prevent the ingredients from sticking. Serve and enjoy.

PORK SHOULDER

Everyone loves some good and juicy pork. Did you know that you can make one in an air fryer? It will be crispy and delicious – perfect for entertaining or just for an amazing dinner or lunch with your spouse.

PREPARATION TIME: 10 MINUTES | **COOKING TIME: 30 MINUTES**

SERVING SIZE: 2 PEOPLE | **PER SERVING: KCAL: 755; FAT: 56G; CARBS: 0.6G; PROTEIN: 58.4G; SUGARS: 0.1G; FIBRE: 0.4G**

Ingredients:

- 500g pork shoulder
- Salt and pepper to taste
- 1 tablespoon white wine vinegar
- 1 teaspoon dried rosemary
- 1 teaspoon olive oil
- 1 teaspoon Dijon mustard

Instructions:

Step 1: First, pat dry the pork shoulder with kitchen paper.
Step 2: Season the pork shoulder with salt and pepper to taste and drizzle with white wine vinegar, dried rosemary, olive oil and mustard.
Step 3: Rub all the ingredients into the meat and place the whole piece of meat in an air fryer basket.
Step 4: Cook for about 20 minutes at 180 C degrees. Then flip the meat on the other side and cook for 10 more minutes. Serve and enjoy with cooked rice, mashed potatoes, or steamed veggies.

SOY SAUCE PORK BITES

Soy sauce and pork meat are one of the matches made in heaven. You will adore this recipe as much as my family does.

PREPARATION TIME: 10 MINUTES | **COOKING TIME: 17-18 MINUTES**

SERVING SIZE: 2 PEOPLE | **PER SERVING: KCAL: 637; FAT: 34.8G; CARBS: 7.1G; PROTEIN: 69.54G; SUGARS: 5.1G; FIBRE: 0.2G**

Ingredients:

- 500g pork loin
- Salt and pepper to taste
- 1 tablespoon brown sugar
- 2 tablespoons soya sauce
- 1 tablespoon sriracha sauce
- 1 garlic clove, minced
- 1 teaspoon onion powder

Instructions:

Step 1: First, pat dry the pork loin and dice it into small bites around 1 cm big.
Step 2: In a medium-sized bowl, mix the brown sugar, soy sauce, sriracha sauce, minced garlic clove, and onion powder.
Step 3: Season the pork pieces with salt and pepper to taste and toss them into the bowl with soy sauce and other ingredients.
Step 4: Place the pork pieces in an air fryer basket.
Step 5: Cook for about 17-18 minutes at 170°C. Shake the air fryer basket halfway through cooking and serve to enjoy.

CHICKEN WITH BRUSSELS SPROUTS

I love juicy chicken. This goes great with brussels sprouts on side.

PREPARATION TIME: 10 MINUTES | **COOKING TIME: 20 MINUTES**

SERVING SIZE: 2 PEOPLE | **PER SERVING: KCAL: 362; FAT: 9.1G; CARBS: 11.9G; PROTEIN: 57.4G; SUGARS: 2.8G; FIBRE: 5G**

Ingredients:

- 500g chicken breast, boneless and skinless (should be about 2 chicken breasts)
- Salt and pepper to taste
- 1 teaspoon dried oregano
- 1 teaspoon chilli flakes
- 1 teaspoon olive oil
- 250g Brussels sprouts

Instructions:

Step 1: First, cut the chicken breasts half to make four chicken fillets.
Step 2: Season them with salt and pepper to taste and dried oregano.
Step 3: Transfer the chicken fillets in an air fryer basket and add in the Brussels sprouts.
Step 4: Drizzle with some olive oil and cook at 180°C for about 10 minutes.
Step 5: Shake the air fryer basket to prevent them from sticking and to develop much crispier crust on the chicken. Continue with cooking for 10 minutes more.

JUICY PARMESAN CRUSTED PORK CHOPS

The whole family will enjoy this meal for dinner or lunch. You can never go wrong with pork chops and parmesan cheese.

PREPARATION TIME: 10 MINUTES | **COOKING TIME: 25 MINUTES**
SERVING SIZE: 2 PEOPLE | **PER SERVING:** KCAL: 1000; FAT: 81.5G; CARBS: 0.9G; PROTEIN: 64.3G; SUGARS: 0G; FIBRE: 0G

Ingredients:
- 500g pork chops, boneless
- 1 tablespoon Cajun seasoning
- 50g grated parmesan cheese
- 2 tablespoons olive oil

Instructions:
Step 1: First, pat dry the pork chops with the help of a kitchen paper.
Step 2: Season the pork chops with Cajun seasoning all over the pork chops and coat them well with grated parmesan cheese.
Step 3: Place the pork chops in an air fryer basket. Drizzle some olive oil on top
Step 4: Cook for about 25 minutes at 170ºC. Make sure to flip the pork chops halfway through cooking. Serve and enjoy with air fried potatoes.

MAPLE MUSTARD PORK TENDERLOIN

Once you try this recipe for pork tenderloin, you will adore this flavour combination and will return to this recipe over and over again.

PREPARATION TIME: 10 MINUTES | **COOKING TIME: 25 MINUTES**
SERVING SIZE: 2 PEOPLE | **PER SERVING:** KCAL: 470; FAT: 9.8G; CARBS: 24.9G; PROTEIN: 67G; SUGARS: 20.3G; FIBRE: 0.7G

Ingredients:
- 500g pork tenderloin
- Salt and pepper to taste
- 1 teaspoon paprika powder
- 1 teaspoon onion powder
- ½ teaspoon garlic powder
- 3 tablespoons maple syrup
- 2 teaspoons mustard
- 1 tablespoon Worcestershire sauce
- 1 tablespoon soy sauce

Instructions:
Step 1: First, pat dry the pork tenderloin.
Step 2: In a medium sized bowl, mix the paprika powder, onion powder, garlic powder, maple syrup, mustard, Worcestershire sauce and soy sauce. Mix until combined.
Step 3: Season the pork tenderloin with salt and pepper to taste and drizzle the maple mustard glaze all over the pork meat.
Step 4: Place the glazed pork tenderloin in an air fryer basket.
Step 5: Cook for about 25 minutes at 170ºC. Serve and enjoy with air fried potatoes.

AIR FRYER PORK CHOPS

This recipe will ask for pork chops that are boneless, but you can use with bone too. The difference is that you'll have less mess when you consume this yummy dinner. I like to serve it with mashed potatoes because pork chops and mashed potatoes are classic that never gets old.

PREPARATION TIME: 10 MINUTES | **COOKING TIME: 20 MINUTES**

SERVING SIZE: 2 PEOPLE | **PER SERVING: KCAL: 835; FAT: 65.6G; CARBS: 0.9G; PROTEIN: 56.6G; SUGARS: 0.3; FIBER: 0.3G**

Ingredients:
- 500g pork chops, boneless
- Salt and pepper to taste
- 1 teaspoon mustard
- 1 teaspoon olive oil
- 1 tablespoon Greek yoghurt
- 1 teaspoon Italian seasoning

Instructions:
Step 1: First, pat dry the pork chops with kitchen paper.
Step 2: Season the pork chops with salt and pepper to taste and coat them with Italian seasoning, mustard, olive oil, and Greek yoghurt.
Step 3: Rub all the ingredients into the meat and place the pork chops in an air fryer basket.
Step 4: Cook for about 10 minutes at 180 C degrees. Then flip the meat on the other side and cook for 10 more minutes. Serve and enjoy with cooked rice, mashed potatoes, or steamed veggies.

PORK AND VEGGIES

This next recipe is perfect for everyone's taste. It's diced pork meat combined with diced veggies. It's nutritious, quick to make, and very delicious.

PREPARATION TIME: 10 MINUTES | **COOKING TIME: 20 MINUTES**

SERVING SIZE: 2 PEOPLE | **PER SERVING: KCAL: 827; FAT: 54.1G; CARBS: 20.7G; PROTEIN: 64.2G; SUGARS: 6.7G; FIBER: 6.9G**

Ingredients:
- 500g pork shoulder
- Salt and pepper to taste
- 1 garlic clove, minced
- 1 teaspoon onion powder
- 1 teaspoon dried thyme
- 2 carrots, peeled and diced
- 250g broccoli florets, diced
- 100g brussels sprouts

Instructions:
Step 1: Pat dry the pork shoulder with kitchen paper and dice in 2 cm cubes.
Step 2: Peel the carrots and dice them into small pieces. Halve the Brussels sprouts and place them in a bowl with the carrots.
Step 3: Add in the diced meat, broccoli florets and season with salt and pepper to taste, minced garlic clove, onion powder and dried thyme.
Step 4: Toss everything together and transfer to an air fryer basket.
Step 5: Cook for about 20 minutes at 170°C degrees. Shake the air fryer basket halfway through cooking and serve to enjoy.

PORK WITH MUSHROOMS

You will love this recipe -- not only because it's quick to prepare, but also because it's bursting with flavours.

PREPARATION TIME: 10 MINUTES | **COOKING TIME: 20 MINUTES**

SERVING SIZE: 2 PEOPLE | **PER SERVING: KCAL: 680; FAT: 39.9G; CARBS: 5.9G; PROTEIN: 72.5G; SUGARS: 2.6G; FIBRE: 1.6G**

Ingredients:
- 500g pork loin
- Salt and pepper to taste
- 1 garlic clove, minced
- 1 teaspoon onion powder
- 1 teaspoon dried thyme
- 250g white button mushrooms
- 2 teaspoons olive oil

Instructions:
Step 1: Pat dry the pork loin with kitchen paper and dice in 2 cm cubes.
Step 2: Clean the mushrooms with kitchen paper and dice them in half.
Step 3: Add in the diced mushrooms in a bowl alongside the diced meat, then season with salt and pepper to taste, onion powder, minced garlic clove, dried thyme, and olive oil.
Step 4: Toss everything together and transfer to an air fryer basket.
Step 5: Cook for about 20 minutes at 170°C. Shake the air fryer basket halfway through cooking and serve to enjoy.

HONEY GLAZED PORK RIBS

Are you a pork rib fan? I've got a perfect recipe for you to enjoy. This pork ribs are glazed with ketchup and honey, and they are perfect for Sunday lunch.

PREPARATION TIME: 10 MINUTES | **COOKING TIME: 20 MINUTES**

SERVING SIZE: 2 PEOPLE | **PER SERVING: KCAL: 760; FAT: 44.4G; CARBS: 20.2G; PROTEIN: 66.9G; SUGARS: 18.6G; FIBRE: 0.2G**

Ingredients:
- 500g pork ribs
- Salt and pepper to taste
- 1 garlic clove, minced
- 1 teaspoon onion powder
- 3 tablespoons ketchup
- 1 tablespoon honey
- 1 tablespoon brown sugar

Instructions:
Step 1: First, pat dry the pork ribs with kitchen paper and season them with salt and pepper to taste.
Step 2: In a medium sized bowl, mix the minced garlic clove, onion powder, ketchup, honey, and brown sugar.
Step 3: Brush the pork ribs with the ketchup and honey mixture all the way on both sides.
Step 4: Place the pork ribs in an air fryer basket.
Step 5: Cook for about 20 minutes at 170°C degrees. Shake the air fryer basket halfway through cooking and serve to enjoy.

AIR FRYER PULLED PORK

Did you know that you can make the air fryer pulled pork easily in around 30 minutes? Yes, it's possible and you will love the flavour.

- PREPARATION TIME: **10 MINUTES** | COOKING TIME: **30 MINUTES**
- SERVING SIZE: **2 PEOPLE** | PER SERVING: **KCAL: 852; FAT: 67.5G; CARBS: 0.1G; PROTEIN: 58.2G; SUGARS: 0G; FIBRE: 0G**

Ingredients:

- 500g pork shoulder
- Salt and pepper to taste
- 1 tablespoon white wine vinegar
- 2 tablespoons olive oil

Instructions:

Step 1: First, pat dry the pork shoulder with the help of a kitchen paper.

Step 2: Season the pork shoulder with salt and pepper to taste and white wine vinegar.

Step 3: Place the pork shoulder in an air fryer basket. Drizzle some olive oil on top.

Step 4: Cook for about 25 minutes at 190°C. Make sure to flip the pork chops halfway through cooking.

Step 5: Take out the pork shoulder from the air fryer basket and pull it apart with the help of two forks.

Step 6: Return the pulled pork in the air fryer basket and cook for about 2-3 minutes more at 160°C. Serve and enjoy with mashed potatoes.

CRISPY AIR FRYER PORK BELLY

For all pork belly lovers out there, I am sure you will enjoy this recipe. I love the crispy and juicy pork in an air fryer.

- PREPARATION TIME: **10 MINUTES** | COOKING TIME: **20 MINUTES**
- SERVING SIZE: **2 PEOPLE** | PER SERVING: **KCAL: 759; FAT: 53.5G; CARBS: 7.5G; PROTEIN: 58.5G; SUGARS: 6.6G; FIBRE: 0.2G**

Ingredients:

- 500g pork shoulder
- Salt and pepper to taste
- 1 tablespoon granulated sugar
- ½ teaspoon garlic powder
- 1 teaspoon onion powder

Instructions:

Step 1: First, pat dry the pork belly with the help of a kitchen paper.

Step 2: Season the pork shoulder with salt and pepper to taste, granulated sugar, onion powder, and garlic powder.

Step 3: Place the pork belly in an air fryer basket.

Step 4: Cook for about 20 minutes at 180°C.

Step 5: Take the pork belly out of the air fryer, let it rest for 5 minutes, and cut it into slices. Serve and enjoy.

STEAK BITES

These steak bites are perfect for cosy dinner or fancy lunch with your loved ones. Just double the ingredients to make enough for everyone.

PREPARATION TIME: **10 MINUTES** | COOKING TIME: **15 MINUTES**
SERVING SIZE: **2 PEOPLE** | PER SERVING: **KCAL: 356; FAT: 18.7G; CARBS: 7.1G; PROTEIN: 40.9G; SUGARS: 5.3G; FIBRE: 0.7G**

Ingredients:

- 500g beef sirloin fillet
- Salt and pepper to taste
- 1 teaspoon paprika powder
- 1 teaspoon chilli flakes
- 1 teaspoon dried oregano
- ½ teaspoon garlic powder
- 1 teaspoon onion powder
- 1 teaspoon mustard
- 1 teaspoon sriracha sauce
- 1 tablespoon olive oil

Instructions:

Step 1: First, pat dry the beef sirloin fillet with kitchen paper and dice into 2 cm pieces.

Step 2: Place the beef pieces in a bowl and season with salt and pepper to taste, paprika powder, chilli flakes, dried oregano, garlic powder, onion powder, mustard, sriracha sauce, and mix until everything is combined, and the meat is fully coated.

Step 3: Transfer the beef pieces in an air fryer basket and drizzle some olive oil.

Step 4: Cook for about 15 minutes at 170°C and don't forget to shake the air dryer basket halfway through cooking.

Step 5: Serve with air fried broccoli florets, or mashed potatoes.

AIR FRYER STEAK

This is going to be probably the best steak you had in your life. It's juicy, perfectly cooked, and always a great way to serve delicious dinner for your loved one.

PREPARATION TIME: **10 MINUTES** | COOKING TIME: **15 MINUTES**
SERVING SIZE: **2 PEOPLE** | PER SERVING: **KCAL: 454; FAT: 27.5G; CARBS: 1G; PROTEIN: 48.4G; SUGARS: 0.4G; FIBRE: 0.1G**

Ingredients:

- 2 pieces mignon steaks = fillet
- 2 tablespoons steak seasonings
- 2 tablespoons butter
- 1 teaspoon garlic powder

Instructions:

Step 1: First, pat dry the mignon steaks with the help of a kitchen paper.

Step 2: Season the steak pieces with steak seasoning and spread them well with butter.

Step 3: Sprinkle with garlic powder on top and place them in an air fryer basket.

Step 4: Cook for about 12-15 minutes at 170°C and serve with roasted veggies. Enjoy.

AIR FRYER FLANK STEAK

This flank steak is juicy and perfect for lunch with your spouse. I love to make it this way because it's bursting with flavours and it's quick to prepare.

PREPARATION TIME: **10 MINUTES** | COOKING TIME: **10 MINUTES**
SERVING SIZE: **2 PEOPLE** | PER SERVING: **KCAL: 574; FAT: 27.9G; CARBS: 7G; PROTEIN: 70G; SUGARS:5.2G; FIBRE: 0.6G**

Ingredients:
- 500g flank steak = bavette
- Salt and pepper to taste
- 1 tablespoon brown sugar
- 1 teaspoon onion powder
- 1 teaspoon garlic powder
- 1 teaspoon chilli flakes
- 1 teaspoon paprika powder
- 1 teaspoon dried oregano
- 1 tablespoon olive oil

Instructions:
Step 1: Pat dry the flank steak with the help of a kitchen paper.
Step 2: Season the flank steak with brown sugar, onion powder, garlic powder, chilli flakes, paprika powder, and dried oregano.
Step 3: Place the flank steak in an air fryer basket. Drizzle with olive oil.
Step 4: Cook for about 10 minutes at 180 C degrees.
Step 5: Take out the flank steak from the air fryer and cut it on a cutting board.

JUICY AIR FRYER STEAK

Here is another popular recipe that I want to share with you guys. You will love this steak recipe.

PREPARATION TIME: **10 MINUTES** | COOKING TIME: **15 MINUTES**
SERVING SIZE: **2 PEOPLE** | PER SERVING: **KCAL: 569; FAT: 39.7G; CARBS: 3.8G; PROTEIN: 51G; SUGARS: 2G; FIBRE: 0.6G**

Ingredients:
- 2 pieces New York strip steaks = sirloin
- 1 tablespoon soy sauce
- 2 tablespoons butter
- ½ tablespoon cocoa powder
- 1 teaspoon brown sugar
- 1 teaspoon paprika powder
- ½ teaspoon onion powder
- ½ teaspoon garlic powder

Instructions:
Step 1: First, pat dry the steaks with the help of a kitchen paper.
Step 2: Season the steak pieces with cocoa powder, brown sugar, paprika powder, onion powder, and garlic powder, then spread them well with butter.
Step 3: Place them in an air fryer basket.
Step 4: Cook for about 12-15 minutes at 170°C and serve with roasted veggies. Enjoy.

BEEF AND VEGGIES SKEWERS

You will love these beef skewers. They are easy to put together with simple ingredients, making a complete meal for the whole family.

PREPARATION TIME: 10 MINUTES | **COOKING TIME:** 15 MINUTES
SERVING SIZE: 2 PEOPLE | **PER SERVING:** KCAL: 545; FAT: 16.4G; CARBS: 17.9G; PROTEIN: 78.4G; SUGARS: 10.6G; FIBRE: 3.4G

Ingredients:

- 500g beef sirloin steak
- Salt and pepper to taste
- 1 teaspoon mustard
- 1 teaspoon brown sugar
- 1 teaspoon paprika powder
- ½ teaspoon onion powder
- 1 teaspoon garlic powder
- 1 tablespoon ketchup
- 1 red onion
- 1 red pepper
- 1 green pepper

Instructions:

Step 1: First, pat dry the beef sirloin with kitchen paper and dice into 2 cm pieces.

Step 2: On a cutting board, dice the red onion, and green and red peppers with a knife into 1 cm pieces.

Step 3: Season the beef pieces with salt and pepper to taste, mustard, brown sugar, paprika powder, onion powder, garlic powder, and ketchup. Mix until everything is combined.

Step 4: Take skewers and insert beef pieces, alternating with onion, and red and green pepper slices.

Step 5: Place the beef skewers in an air fryer basket and cook for about 15 minutes at 170°C degrees. Serve and enjoy with tzatziki sauce.

Please scan the QR code below to access your bonus PDF with all 150 recipes with full coloured photos & beautiful designs alongside!

This is the only way we can get the recipes with coloured photos to you & keep the book as reasonably priced as possible.

Also, once downloaded you can take the PDF with you digitally wherever you go- meaning you can cook these recipes wherever you may be! (As long as you have an air fryer!)

We hope you enjoy and do let us know your feedback!

STEP BY STEP GUIDE TO ACCESS

1. Open Your Phones (Or Any Device You Want The Book On) Back Camera. The Back Camera Is The One You use as if you are taking a picture of someone.
2. Simply point your Camera at the QR code and 'tap' the QR code with your finger to focus the camera.
3. A link / pop up will appear. Simply tap that (and make sure you have internet connection) and the FREE PDF containing all of the coloured images should appear.
4. Now you have access to these FOREVER. Simply 'Bookmark' The tab it opened on, or download the document and take wherever you want.
5. Repeat this on any device you want it on! (If you want it on a laptop, simply email the document to yourself!)

VEGAN AND VEGGIES
Recipes
— **10 RECIPES** —

VEGAN SPAGHETTI PIE

This is probably the best way to serve your spaghetti because it is delicious, fancy, and super easy to make.

PREPARATION TIME: **10 MINUTES** | COOKING TIME: **10 MINUTES**
SERVING SIZE: **2 PEOPLE** | PER SERVING: **KCAL: 421; FAT: 5.6G; CARBS: 73.6G; PROTEIN: 19.3G; SUGARS: 3.3G; FIBRE: 1.5G**

Ingredients:

- 250g spaghetti, vegan
- Salt and pepper to taste
- 150 ml tomato sauce
- 100g vegan mozzarella cheese
- 1 teaspoon dried oregano

Instructions:

Step 1: In a pot, bring salted water to a boil and cook the spaghetti al dente.
Step 2: Drain the water from spaghetti and place the spaghetti in a large mixing bowl.
Step 3: Season with salt and pepper to taste, add in the tomato sauce, grated mozzarella cheese, and dried oregano.
Step 4: Mix everything together until fully combined and transfer to a round casserole pan that will fit into your air fryer basket.
Step 5: Cook for about 10 minutes at 180°C degrees.
Step 6: Let it cool slightly and serve to enjoy.

AIR FRYER CRISPY TOFU BURGERS

I love this amazing vegan burger option. You can eat it as it is, place it in burger buns, or just serve it with toasted salad. Yummy and delicious.

PREPARATION TIME: **10 MINUTES** | COOKING TIME: **30 MINUTES**
SERVING SIZE: **2 PEOPLE** | PER SERVING: **KCAL: 255; FAT: 15.4G; CARBS: 14.4G; PROTEIN: 17.7G; SUGARS: 5.7G; FIBRE: 2.1G**

Ingredients:

- 2 200g tofu pieces
- Salt and pepper to taste
- 1 tablespoon soy sauce
- 1 tablespoon brown sugar
- 1 teaspoon paprika powder
- 1 tablespoon olive oil
- 1 tablespoon rice vinegar
- 2 tablespoons all-purpose flour

Instructions:

Step 1: In a bowl, mix the salt and pepper to taste, soy sauce, brown sugar, paprika powder, olive oil, and rice vinegar.
Step 2: Coat the tofu slices in the marinade and drain well.
Step 3: Coat the tofu slices with all-purpose flour and arrange them in an air fryer basket.
Step 4: Spray with cooking spray and cook for about 15 minutes. Make sure to flip the tofu slices halfway through cooking and serve to enjoy.

CHERRY TOMATOES WITH BASIL DRESSING

This is perfect vegan warm salad that will absolutely blow your mind by how delicious it is.

PREPARATION TIME: 10 MINUTES | **COOKING TIME: 5 MINUTES**

SERVING SIZE: 2 PEOPLE | **PER SERVING: KCAL: 168; FAT: 14.6G; CARBS: 10.3G; PROTEIN: 2.4G; SUGARS: 6.6G; FIBRE: 3.4G**

Ingredients:
- 500g grape tomatoes
- Salt and pepper to taste
- 1 teaspoon dried oregano
- 2 tablespoons freshly chopped basil
- 2 tablespoons olive oil

Instructions:
Step 1: First, cut the grape tomatoes in half with a knife.
Step 2: Transfer the tomato halves to a large mixing bowl and season with salt and pepper to taste.
Step 3: Season with dried oregano and freshly chopped basil, then drizzle the olive oil.
Step 4: Mix and toss everything together and transfer to an air fryer basket.
Step 5: Cook for about 5 minutes at 180°C. Serve and enjoy.

TOASTED VEGGIES

If you love your veggies, then you can consider this a whole lunch, and you won't regret a bite!

PREPARATION TIME: 10 MINUTES | **COOKING TIME: 10 MINUTES**

SERVING SIZE: 2 PEOPLE | **PER SERVING: KCAL: 268; FAT: 15.4G; CARBS: 31.9G; PROTEIN: 6.3G; SUGARS: 12.6G; FIBRE: 8.1G**

Ingredients:
- 1 green bell pepper
- 1 red bell pepper
- 1 yellow pepper
- 200g brussels sprouts
- 1 red onion
- 2 carrots, peeled
- 1 stalk of leek
- Salt and pepper to taste
- 1 teaspoon Italian seasoning
- 2 tablespoons olive oil
- 1 tablespoon soy sauce

Instructions:
Step 1: On a cutting board, cut the bell peppers into 1-2 cm pieces. Cut the brussels sprouts in half, dice the red onion, dice the peeled carrots, and dice the leek into small pieces.
Step 2: Transfer them all into a large mixing bowl and season with salt and pepper to taste.
Step 3: Season with Italian seasoning, olive oil, and soy sauce.
Step 4: Mix and toss everything together and transfer to an air fryer basket.
Step 5: Cook for about 10 minutes at 180°C. Serve and enjoy.

ROASTED BROCCOLI WITH GARLIC VINAIGRETTE

You will love these roasted broccoli florets with garlic vinaigrette. They are a quick and perfect addition to your main meal. Serve with steak, chicken, or pork. You can enjoy them as they are too!

PREPARATION TIME: **10 MINUTES** | COOKING TIME: **10 MINUTES**
SERVING SIZE: **2 PEOPLE** | PER SERVING: **KCAL: 154; FAT: 7.9G; CARBS: 18.2G; PROTEIN: 7.3G; SUGARS: 4.3G; FIBRE: 6.9G**

Ingredients:
- 500g broccoli florets
- Salt and pepper to taste
- 1 tablespoon white wine vinegar
- 1 tablespoon olive oil
- 2 garlic cloves, minced
- 1 teaspoon dried oregano
- 1 teaspoon Herbs de Provence

Instructions:
Step 1: In a large mixing bowl, place the broccoli florets and season \ with salt and pepper to taste.
Step 2: Season with white wine vinegar, olive oil, minced garlic cloves, dried oregano and herbs de Provence.
Step 3: Mix and toss everything together and transfer to an air fryer basket.
Step 4: Cook for about 10 minutes at 180°C. Serve and enjoy.

PEANUT BUTTER CAULIFLOWER BITES

These peanut butter cauliflower bites are absolutely amazing and easy to put together.

PREPARATION TIME: **10 MINUTES** | COOKING TIME: **10 MINUTES**
SERVING SIZE: **2 PEOPLE** | PER SERVING: **KCAL: 217; FAT: 15.3G; CARBS: 16.4G; PROTEIN: 9G; SUGARS: 7.5G; FIBRE: 7.2G**

Ingredients:
- 500g cauliflower florets
- Salt and pepper to taste
- 2 tablespoons peanut butter, runny
- 1 tablespoon olive oil
- 1 teaspoon paprika powder

Instructions:
Step 1: Place the cauliflower florets in a large mixing bowl and season with salt and pepper to taste.
Step 2: Pour in the peanut butter, olive oil, and paprika powder.
Step 3: Mix and toss everything together and transfer to an air fryer basket.
Step 4: Cook for about 10 minutes at 180°C. Serve and enjoy.

KALE AND POTATO NUGGETS

This is a healthy chicken nuggets alternative. Vegan version that you are going to love. It's quite easy to prepare.

PREPARATION TIME: 10 MINUTES | **COOKING TIME: 10 MINUTES**

SERVING SIZE: 2 PEOPLE | **PER SERVING: KCAL: 342; FAT: 7.4G; CARBS: 63.7G; PROTEIN: 7.8G; SUGARS: 4.3G; FIBRE: 9.7G**

Ingredients:
- 2 large potatoes
- Salt and pepper to taste
- 100g kale, chopped
- 1 tablespoon olive oil
- 1 garlic clove, minced
- 1 teaspoon paprika powder

Instructions:
Step 1: In a pot, bring salted water to a boil and cook the potatoes until fork tender. It will take around 20 minutes.
Step 2: Drain the potatoes well, mash them with a fork, and season with salt and pepper to taste, minced garlic clove, and paprika powder.
Step 3: Chop up your kale into fine strips and stir it in the potato mixture.
Step 4: Form small nugget-shaped pieces and arrange them in an air fryer basket.
Step 5: Cook for about 10 minutes at 180°C. Enjoy!

BUFFALO CAULIFLOWER

This is one of the best buffalo cauliflower crunchy florets you will ever have. They are easy and quite quick to put together.

PREPARATION TIME: 10 MINUTES | **COOKING TIME: 15 MINUTES**

SERVING SIZE: 2 PEOPLE | **PER SERVING: KCAL: 292; FAT: 16.4G; CARBS: 15.3G; PROTEIN: 3.5G; SUGARS: 3.2G; FIBRE: 5.1G**

Ingredients:
- 1 cauliflower head, cut into florets
- Salt and pepper to taste
- 100g buffalo sauce, vegan
- 60g panko breadcrumbs
- 2 tablespoons olive oil

Instructions:
Step 1: In a large mixing bowl, add in the cauliflower florets.
Step 2: Season with salt and pepper to taste and buffalo sauce. Toss everything together until the florets are fully coated.
Step 3: Sprinkle with Panko breadcrumbs on top and shake so they will stick evenly on the florets.
Step 4: Transfer the cauliflower florets in an air fryer basket and drizzle with some olive oil on top.
Step 5: Cook for about 15 minutes at 180°C and serve to enjoy.

GREEN BEANS WITH GARLIC MUSTARD DRESSING

A perfect side dish that will absolutely keep you refreshed and healthy during the holiday season.

PREPARATION TIME: 10 MINUTES | **COOKING TIME: 10 MINUTES**

SERVING SIZE: 2 PEOPLE | **PER SERVING: KCAL: 114; FAT: 1.7G; CARBS: 20.2G; PROTEIN: 7.2G; SUGARS: 8.8G; FIBRE: 9.5G**

Ingredients:

- 500g green beans, fresh or frozen
- Salt and pepper to taste
- 1 tablespoon apple cider vinegar
- 1 tablespoon mustard
- 1 teaspoon honey
- 2 garlic cloves, minced
- 1 teaspoon dried oregano

Instructions:

Step 1: In a large mixing bowl, place the green beans and season with salt and pepper to taste.

Step 2: Season with apple cider vinegar, mustard, honey, minced garlic cloves, and dried oregano.

Step 3: Mix and toss everything together and transfer to an air fryer basket.

Step 4: Cook for about 10 minutes at 180°C. Serve and enjoy.

CRISPY TOFU

This crispy tofu recipe is amazingly delicious, quick, and perfect for vegans and vegetarians.

PREPARATION TIME: 10 MINUTES | **COOKING TIME: 10 MINUTES**

SERVING SIZE: 2 PEOPLE | **PER SERVING: KCAL: 251; FAT: 17G; CARBS: 11.7G; PROTEIN: 17.9G; SUGARS: 7.7G; FIBRE: 2.7G**

Ingredients:

- 400g tofu
- Salt and pepper to taste
- 1 tablespoon olive oil
- 1 tablespoon brown sugar
- 1 tablespoon sriracha sauce
- 1 tablespoon mustard
- 1 tablespoon ketchup

Instructions:

Step 1: First, in a large mixing bowl mix the olive oil, brown sugar, sriracha sauce, mustard, ketchup and salt and pepper to taste.

Step 2: On a cutting board, dice the tofu into 1 cm cubes and add them to the sauce mixture.

Step 3: Coat well and let it steep for 2-3 minutes.

Step 4: Transfer the marinated tofu in an air fryer basket and cook for about 10 minutes at 180°C.

Step 5: Serve with fresh salad, tahini sauce, or cooked basmati rice.

Please scan the QR code below to access your bonus PDF with all 150 recipes with full coloured photos & beautiful designs alongside!

This is the only way we can get the recipes with coloured photos to you & keep the book as reasonably priced as possible.

Also, once downloaded you can take the PDF with you digitally wherever you go- meaning you can cook these recipes wherever you may be! (As long as you have an air fryer!)

We hope you enjoy and do let us know your feedback!

STEP BY STEP GUIDE TO ACCESS

1. Open Your Phones (Or Any Device You Want The Book On) Back Camera. The Back Camera Is The One You use as if you are taking a picture of someone.
2. Simply point your Camera at the QR code and 'tap' the QR code with your finger to focus the camera.
3. A link / pop up will appear. Simply tap that (and make sure you have internet connection) and the FREE PDF containing all of the coloured images should appear.
4. Now you have access to these FOREVER. Simply 'Bookmark' The tab it opened on, or download the document and take wherever you want.
5. Repeat this on any device you want it on! (If you want it on a laptop, simply email the document to yourself!)

DESSERTS
Recipes
— 15 RECIPES —

MINI APPLE PIES

These are delicious mini alternatives to traditional apple pies.

PREPARATION TIME: 10 MINUTES | **COOKING TIME: 10 MINUTES**

SERVING SIZE: 6 | **PER SERVING: KCAL: 325; FAT: 16.8G; CARBS: 40.3G; PROTEIN: 4.3G; SUGARS: 16.5G; FIBRE: 2.7G**

Ingredients:

- 250g puff pastry
- 2 apples, peeled and diced
- 50g granulated sugar
- 1 teaspoon ground cinnamon
- 2 tablespoons cornstarch
- 1 teaspoon vanilla extract
- 1 large egg, lightly whisked

Instructions:

Step 1: First, roll out the puff pastry on a lightly floured surface. Cut 7 cm diameter round shapes with the help of glass and set them aside.

Step 2: Peel the apples and grate them finely on a kitchen grater. Place them in a mixing bowl.

Step 3: In the same bowl, add the granulated sugar, cornstarch, ground cinnamon, and vanilla extract.

Step 4: Add a small amount of the apple filling to one piece of dough and cover it with another piece of dough. Seal the edges with the help of a fork.

Step 5: Whisk the egg lightly in a small bowl and brush each pie with it.

Step 6: Transfer 4 apple pies to the air fryer basket and cook for about 15 minutes at 190°C until puffed up.

Step 7: Serve them with icing sugar and enjoy.

EASY BROWNIES

Did you know that you can prepare brownies in an air fryer? They are super easy and very delicious to make.

PREPARATION TIME: 10 MINUTES | **COOKING TIME: 15 MINUTES**

SERVING SIZE: 4 PEOPLE | **PER SERVING: KCAL: 279; FAT: 6.9G; CARBS: 53.1G; PROTEIN: 5.9G; SUGARS: 38G; FIBRE: 2.4G**

Ingredients:

- 60g all-purpose flour
- 5 tablespoons cocoa powder
- 150g granulated sugar
- 2 large eggs, room temperature
- 1 teaspoon vanilla extract
- 1 tablespoon vegetable oil
- Pinch of salt
- ¼ teaspoon baking powder

Instructions:

Step 1: In a large mixing bowl, mix the flour, cocoa powder, and baking powder.

Step 2: In another bowl, mix the granulated sugar, eggs, vanilla extract, and vegetable oil.

Step 3: Mix the dry ingredients into the wet ingredients, then pour the mixture into a greased casserole pan that can fit into your air fryer basket.

Step 4: Cook for about 15 minutes at 180°C. Let it cool slightly and cut it into slices.

BAKED APPLES

Light and easy dessert idea that you can prepare for four servings at a time. You will love some drizzled honey on top or whipped cream for extra flavour.

⏱ PREPARATION TIME: **10 MINUTES** | 🍲 COOKING TIME: **15 MINUTES**

🍽 SERVING SIZE: **2 PEOPLE** | PER SERVING: **KCAL: 737; FAT: 27.1G; CARBS: 112.9G; PROTEIN: 10.7G; SUGARS: 42.8G; FIBRE: 7.7G**

Ingredients:

- 4 apples
- 8 tablespoons ground tea biscuits
- 3 tablespoons melted butter
- 1 tablespoon granulated sugar
- 1 teaspoon ground cinnamon
- 2 tablespoons honey

Instructions:

Step 1: First, core the apples in the centre, removing the seeds and making a hole.
Step 2: Place the apples in an air fryer and cook for about 10 minutes at 180°C.
Step 3: In a large mixing bowl, mix the ground tea biscuits, melted butter, granulated sugar, and ground cinnamon.
Step 4: Take out the baked apples and fill the centres with the ground biscuit mixture.
Step 5: Bake for 5 more minutes at 180°C and serve with a drizzle of honey.

APPLE FRITTERS

These are a healthier donut alternative, and you will love every bite.

⏱ PREPARATION TIME: **10 MINUTES** | 🍲 COOKING TIME: **15 MINUTES**

🍽 SERVING SIZE: **2 PEOPLE** | PER SERVING: **KCAL: 647; FAT: 7.6G; CARBS: 130.3G; PROTEIN: 17.6G; SUGARS: 51.3G; FIBRE: 8.6G**

Ingredients:

- 180g all-purpose flour
- 50g granulated sugar
- 2 teaspoons baking powder
- Pinch of salt
- 1 teaspoon ground cinnamon
- 80 ml whole milk
- 1 teaspoon vanilla extract
- 2 large eggs, room temperature
- 2 apples, peeled and diced

Instructions:

Step 1: In a large mixing bowl, mix the flour, granulated sugar, baking powder, salt, ground cinnamon, whole milk, vanilla extract, and eggs.
Step 2: Peel and dice the apples into small pieces and stir them into the fritter batter.
Step 3: Line your air fryer basket with a piece of parchment paper.
Step 4: Drop 2-3 tablespoons of the apple fritter batter and spray with cooking spray.
Step 5: Air fry the apple fritters at 200°C for about 2-3 minutes.
Step 6: Flip on the other side and cook for 2-3 minutes more.
Step 7: Serve with icing sugar on top.

CHOCOLATE MUFFINS

All you need to make these muffins are silicon muffin moulds, and you will absolutely enjoy their flavour.

PREPARATION TIME: 10 MINUTES | **COOKING TIME: 15 MINUTES**

SERVING SIZE: 4 PEOPLE | **PER SERVING: KCAL: 680; FAT: 25.3G; CARBS: 106.6G; PROTEIN: 15.9G; SUGARS: 48.1G; FIBRE: 7.4G**

Ingredients:

- 240 ml whole milk
- 1 teaspoon white vinegar
- 250g all-purpose flour
- 70g cocoa powder
- 2 teaspoons baking powder
- 150g granulated sugar
- 2 large eggs, room temperature
- Pinch of salt
- 70g melted butter
- 2 teaspoons vanilla extract
- 50g chocolate chips

Instructions:

Step 1: In a large mixing bowl, mix the whole milk, white vinegar, granulated sugar, eggs, salt, melted butter, and vanilla extract.
Step 2: Stir in the flour, cocoa powder, baking powder, and salt.
Step 3: Mix until combined and fold in the chocolate chips.
Step 4: Divide the muffin batter into silicone moulds and cook in an air fryer basket for about 15 minutes at 180°C.
Step 5: Let them cool completely and serve with icing sugar.

BEST PEANUT BUTTER EXPLOSION CAKES

I love these amazing peanut butter explosion cakes. They are delicious, quick, and easy to put together.

PREPARATION TIME: 10 MINUTES | **COOKING TIME: 15 MINUTES**

SERVING SIZE: 4 PEOPLE | **PER SERVING: KCAL: 637; FAT: 43.7G; CARBS: 56.4G; PROTEIN: 12.2G; SUGARS: 39.4G; FIBRE: 5.1G**

Ingredients:

- 120g butter, softened
- 100g powdered sugar
- 100g chocolate chips
- 2 large eggs
- 1 teaspoon vanilla extract
- 40g cocoa powder
- 40g all-purpose flour
- Pinch of salt
- 4 tablespoons peanut butter

Instructions:

Step 1: In a large mixing bowl, place the butter and chocolate chips.
Step 2: Microwave until fully melted. It will take around 2 minutes.
Step 3: In the same bowl, stir in the powdered sugar, eggs, vanilla extract, cocoa powder, salt, and flour.
Step 4: Mix until everything is combined and transfer the batter halfway through in four well-greased ramekins.
Step 5: Add 1 tablespoon of peanut butter in each ramekin and fill up with rest of the chocolate batter.
Step 6: Air fry for about 15 minutes at 180°C.
Step 7: Let them cool slightly and flip them on serving plate. Dust with icing sugar and enjoy.

COOKIES

Did you know that you can prepare cookies in an air fryer? You will adore them because they are fresh, quick and fun to make.

PREPARATION TIME: 10 MINUTES | **COOKING TIME: 15 MINUTES**
SERVING SIZE: 12 PEOPLE | **PER SERVING:** CAL: 235; FAT: 13.6G; CARBS: 25.2G; PROTEIN: 3.8G; SUGARS: 12.7G; FIBRE: 1G

Ingredients:
- 120g butter, softened
- 50g light brown sugar
- 50g granulated sugar
- 1 large egg
- 1 teaspoon vanilla extract
- 180g all-purpose flour
- Pinch of salt
- ½ teaspoon baking soda
- 100g chocolate chips
- 50g walnuts, chopped

Instructions:
Step 1: In a large mixing bowl, beat the butter with the light brown sugar and granulated sugar.
Step 2: Stir in the egg and vanilla extract and mix until combined.
Step 3: Stir in the flour, salt, and baking soda, and mix until just combined.
Step 4: Stir in the chocolate chips and chopped walnuts.
Step 5: Line a piece of parchment paper into your air fryer basket and add tablespoonfuls of the cookie batter.
Step 6: Make sure to add 2-3 at a time and cook at 180°C for about 10 minutes.
Step 7: Remove the cookies and repeat with the rest of the batter. Serve and enjoy.

AIR FRYER CHURROS

These air fryer churros are everything you need on a busy working day when you crave something to satisfy your sweet tooth.

PREPARATION TIME: 10 MINUTES | **COOKING TIME: 15 MINUTES**
SERVING SIZE: 2 PEOPLE | **PER SERVING:** KCAL: 654; FAT: 38.1G; CARBS: 65G; PROTEIN: 13.5G; SUGARS: 12.9G; FIBRE: 3.6G

Ingredients:
- 240 ml water
- 80g butter, melted
- 130g all-purpose flour
- 2 tablespoons granulated sugar
- Pinch of salt
- 2 large eggs, room temperature
- 1 teaspoon vanilla extract
- 100g granulated sugar
- 1 tablespoon ground cinnamon

Instructions:
Step 1: In a saucepan bring the water and butter to a boil.
Step 2: Stir in the sugar, salt, and flour and mix until a dough-like consistency is formed.
Step 3: Remove the saucepan from the heat and stir in the eggs, mixing well between each addition.
Step 4: Transfer the dough into a piping bag fitted with a large star tip.
Step 5: Place a piece of parchment paper into your air fryer basket and pipe out 4-5 churros at a time.
Step 6: Cook at 180°C for about 10-12 minutes.
Step 7: Mix the granulated sugar and cinnamon together and coat the churros in the cinnamon sugar. Serve and enjoy.

PANCAKES

If you are in a hurry, these pancakes are perfect for everyone's taste. Your kids will especially enjoy these.

PREPARATION TIME: 10 MINUTES | **COOKING TIME: 15 MINUTES**

SERVING SIZE: 2 PEOPLE | **PER SERVING: KCAL: 317; FAT: 4.8G; CARBS: 54.8G; PROTEIN: 12.7G; SUGARS: 8.9G; FIBRE: 1.6**

Ingredients:
- 250g pancake mix
- 360 ml buttermilk
- Cooking spray

Instructions:
Step 1: First, place the pancake mix in a large mixing bowl.
Step 2: Stir in the buttermilk and mix until combined.
Step 3: Place a piece of parchment paper into your air fryer basket and spray it with cooking spray.
Step 4: Add two tablespoonfuls of your pancake batter and cook at 180°C for about 3-4 minutes.
Step 5: Flip on the other side and cook for 1-2 minutes more.
Step 6: Serve with icing sugar and a drizzle of maple syrup or honey to enjoy.

AIR-FRIED BANANAS

Quick and easy dessert recipe that can be consumed as is or topped over ice cream. You can also serve these caramelized bananas with whipped cream if you like.

PREPARATION TIME: 10 MINUTES | **COOKING TIME: 15 MINUTES**

SERVING SIZE: 2 PEOPLE | **PER SERVING: KCAL: 176; FAT: 6.2G; CARBS: 32.3G; PROTEIN: 1.4G; SUGARS: 18.8G; FIBRE: 3.7G**

Ingredients:
- 2 bananas, peeled
- 1 tablespoon butter, melted
- 1 tablespoon brown sugar
- 1 teaspoon ground cinnamon

Instructions:
Step 1: Peel the bananas and slice in half.
Step 2: Arrange the banana pieces in an air fryer basket lined with a piece of parchment paper.
Step 3: Sprinkle some brown sugar on top and sprinkle with ground cinnamon.
Step 4: Cook for about 7-8 minutes at 190°C.
Step 5: Serve with icing sugar on top and enjoy. You can also serve on top of ice cream or with a dollop of whipped cream.

AIR-FRIED OREOS

With only two ingredients, enjoy this amazing dessert with your whole family. I love to make them with my kids.

- **PREPARATION TIME: 10 MINUTES**
- **COOKING TIME: 15 MINUTES**
- **SERVING SIZE: 2 PEOPLE**
- **PER SERVING: KCAL: 265; FAT: 11.6G; CARBS: 37.7G; PROTEIN: 3.4G; SUGARS: 19.3G; FIBRE: 1.3G**

Ingredients:
- 9 Oreo cookies
- 1 sheet crescent rolls

Instructions:
Step 1: First, roll out the crescent roll on a lightly floured working surface.
Step 2: Cut circles slightly bigger than an Oreo cookie.
Step 3: Wrap the crescent dough all over each Oreo and place the wrapped Oreo cookies in an air fryer basket.
Step 4: Cook for about 10 minutes at 180°C.
Step 5: Serve with icing sugar and enjoy.

CARAMELIZED PINEAPPLE

You will absolutely adore these caramelized pineapple slices, and you can serve them just like they are or place them on top of your ice cream. They go well with whipped cream too.

- **PREPARATION TIME: 10 MINUTES**
- **COOKING TIME: 15 MINUTES**
- **SERVING SIZE: 2 PEOPLE**
- **PER SERVING: KCAL: 202; FAT: 0.7G; CARBS: 52.6G; PROTEIN: 1.8G; SUGARS: 41.2G; FIBRE: 4.9G**

Ingredients:
- 4 pineapple slices
- 2 tablespoons brown sugar
- Cooking spray
- ½ teaspoon cinnamon

Instructions:
Step 1: In a bowl, mix the brown sugar and cinnamon together.
Step 2: Arrange the pineapple slices in an air fryer basket lined with a piece of parchment paper.
Step 3: Spray with a little bit of cooking spray. Sprinkle the cinnamon sugar mixture on top.
Step 4: Air fry for about 6 minutes at 180°C.
Step 5: Serve on top of ice cream or with whipped cream.

HAND JAM PIES

With this recipe, you can use your favourite pie dough, or you can use store-bought puff pastry. They are delicious, crispy, and amazing.

PREPARATION TIME: 10 MINUTES | **COOKING TIME: 15 MINUTES**

SERVING SIZE: 2 PEOPLE | **PER SERVING: KCAL: 946; FAT: 49.9G; CARBS: 112.6G; PROTEIN: 12.2G; SUGARS: 41.9G; FIBRE: 2.7G**

Ingredients:
- 250g puff pastry
- 150g cherry jam
- 1 egg, lightly whisked
- 1-2 tablespoons brown sugar

Instructions:
Step 1: First, roll out the puff pastry on a lightly floured working surface.
Step 2: Cut circles from the dough that are 7-8 cm in diameter.
Step 3: Place some of the cherry jam in the middle of each circle, then close the pies, sealing the edges with a fork.
Step 4: Transfer the hand pies to an air fryer basket and brush them with a little bit of lightly whisked egg.
Step 5: Cook in an air fryer for about 15 minutes at 180°C.
Step 6: Serve with a dusting of icing sugar.

AIR FRYER CRONUTS

I love to make donuts, but this time I am bringing them a level up to make them crunchier and tastier than ever.

PREPARATION TIME: 10 MINUTES | **COOKING TIME: 15 MINUTES**

SERVING SIZE: 2 PEOPLE | **PER SERVING: KCAL: 759; FAT: 47.6G; CARBS: 75.3G; PROTEIN: 9.2G; SUGARS: 19G; FIBRE: 2.5G**

Ingredients:
- 250g puff pastry
- 3 tablespoons granulated sugar
- 1 teaspoon ground cinnamon

Instructions:
Step 1: First, roll out the puff pastry on a lightly floured working surface.
Step 2: Cut the donuts with the help of a glass. Line the air fryer basket with parchment paper, then place two to three pieces in the air fryer basket.
Step 3: Cook for about 15 minutes at 190°C.
Step 4: As soon as the cronuts are done cooking, roll them in granulated sugar and cinnamon mixed together.

AIR FRYER APPLE FRIES

These healthy apple snacks are the perfect dessert to serve your guests.

PREPARATION TIME: 10 MINUTES | **COOKING TIME: 15 MINUTES**

SERVING SIZE: 2 PEOPLE | **PER SERVING: KCAL: 663; FAT: 11.1G; CARBS: 128.4G; PROTEIN: 16.5G; SUGARS: 51G; FIBRE: 10.4G**

Ingredients:

- 3 apples, peeled
- 2 large eggs, lightly whisked
- 100g all-purpose flour
- 100g ground biscuits
- 1 tablespoon granulated sugar

Instructions:

Step 1: First, lightly whisked the eggs and place them in a bowl.
Step 2: Peel and dice the apples and coat them in all-purpose flour.
Step 3: Dip each slice of apple in the egg mixture and coat well with the ground cookies and granulated sugar mixed.
Step 4: Arrange the apple slices in an air fryer basket lined with a piece of parchment paper.
Step 5: Cook for about 7 minutes at 180ºC.
Step 6: Serve and enjoy.

Printed in Great Britain
by Amazon